stepping twice

into the river

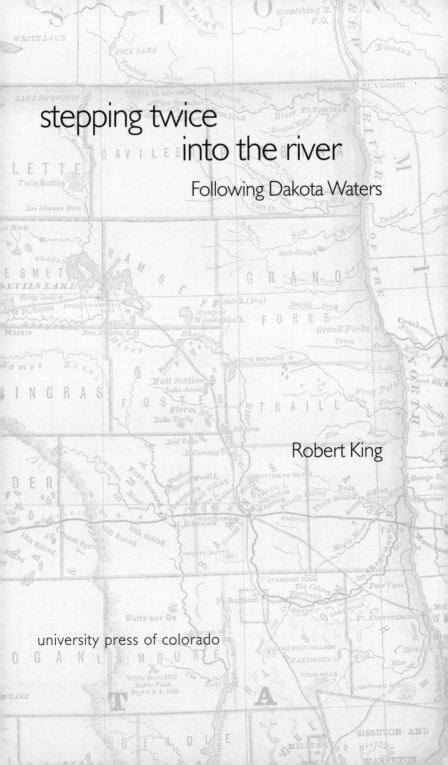

stepping twice
into the river
Following Dakota Waters

Robert King

university press of colorado

Published by the University Press of Colorado
5589 Arapahoe Avenue, Suite 206C
Boulder, Colorado 80303

All rights reserved
Printed in the United States of America

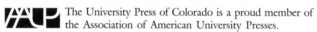 The University Press of Colorado is a proud member of
the Association of American University Presses.

The University Press of Colorado is a cooperative publishing enterprise
supported, in part, by Adams State College, Colorado State University, Fort
Lewis College, Mesa State College, Metropolitan State College of Denver,
University of Colorado, University of Northern Colorado, and Western State
College of Colorado.

The paper used in this publication meets the minimum requirements of the
American National Standard for Information Sciences—Permanence of
Paper for Printed Library Materials. ANSI Z39.48-1992

Library of Congress Cataloging-in-Publication Data

King, Robert, 1937 Dec. 7–
  Stepping twice into the river : following Dakota waters / Robert King.
    p. cm.
  Includes bibliographical references.
  ISBN 0-87081-791-4 (alk. paper) — ISBN 0-87081-792-2 (pbk. : alk. paper)
    1. Sheyenne River Region (N.D.)—History, Local. 2. River life—North
Dakota—Sheyenne River Region—History. 3. Sheyenne River Region
(N.D.)—Description and travel. 4. King, Robert, 1937 Dec. 7– —Travel—
North Dakota—Sheyenne River Region. I. Title.
F642.S53K56 2005
978.4'76—dc22

                                                                2005003913

Design by Daniel Pratt

14 13 12 11 10 09 08 07 06 05   10 9 8 7 6 5 4 3 2 1

Portions of the present work appeared in a slightly different version in the
following publications: "A Circle of Land," *Ascent* 28:12 (Winter 2004); "Grass
Land Water," *South Dakota Review* 38:2 (Summer 2000); "Lost at Home in
the Bottomlands," *Weber Studies: voices and viewpoints of the contemporary west*
20:3 (Spring–Summer 2003); "Valley Home," *North Dakota Quarterly* 65:4
(Winter 1998); "With Nicollet and Heraclitus on the Sheyenne," *Arkansas
Review* 28:2 (August 1997).

To all Dakotans who share
in the past, present, and future of the territory
and to Elizabeth Franklin and my children,
Lisa, Lynn, and Lawrence.

contents

A few years ago, in late autumn, I stood beside the center of the North American continent. It had turned out to be a small prairie pothole lake in North Dakota, that "large rectangular blank spot in the nation's mind," as native son Eric Sevaried once said. A few frogs croaked from the reeds along the edge, the only sound, and a few ducks V-shaped it over the placid surface, the only movement. An almost imperceptible lift in all directions kept the lake in its shallow bowl.

I'd come because I was attracted by the certainty of the Pierce County plat book's official red star in the middle of an unnamed lake—not the cobbled monument at a convenient intersection in Rugby a few miles away—and I was here. I listened to the frogs and waited, maybe for someone to come bouncing along in a pickup although no one did.

I'd wanted to explore a landscape I'd become familiar with for twenty-three years because I was getting ready to leave, suspended between two places and two lives. My former wife lived here, my three children, none born here, had settled in three towns, and my second wife had left to begin a new job in another state where I'd join her after one last year of teaching the future, preparing education students for their elementary classrooms. I was retiring a little early from one way of life and didn't know what the next one would be. We sold the house and I moved into a fifth-floor apartment in downtown Grand Forks overlooking the Red River. I wanted to use that year to discover something and had picked this lake first, thrilled at being in the center of something.

But where else was I? In one way, Nowhere. Dakota is a blank for some because it's too far inland, too far to the north, and lacks the instant icons of other states—no Liberty Bell, Disneyland, snow-capped Rockies—as well as those defining historical moments—no Civil War, Gold Rush, smoke pouring from industrial chimneys as America becomes itself.

But Nowhere can expand itself to Anywhere. In every highway cafe in Dakota you might not know if you were in Texas or Nebraska, Kansas or Wyoming. The same winds of climate and politics blow across the plains, and the same human nature contributes to progress and blocks it, praises it, and complains about it—especially in the highway cafe.

And Anywhere also transforms itself. As Thom McGrath, Dakota-born poet, wrote, "North Dakota is Everywhere."

Understood, misunderstood, looking wise, looking silly, the line—written in Greece about the suicide of an impoverished fisherman—has to do with Dakota as a *condition*. Other places,

McGrath writes, are part of this same condition, "so long as it is not the East, the city."

I stood that day in the middle of Everywhere, the scene stunningly ordinary but almost fragile. The sky's blue grew thinner, as if something were wearing away above. The clouds seemed wispier, the water a lighter glaze than before. I felt as if the whole picture might thin and disappear, winking out and pulling me along, lighter, airier, a ghost lake with a ghostly watcher. I waited to see what would change and everything stayed the same. After five more minutes, I walked back to my car.

Driving, I vaguely wondered what else I might visit my last year, and then it happened. I found myself following the small Sheyenne River calmly moving east when it struck me that I'd crossed it, in my casual traveling, moving south as well as north. I wondered how it had gotten in all directions and, that night, spread out a map.

The Sheyenne began near the middle of North Dakota, ran through farmland as the boundary of a Sioux reservation, then curved south almost halfway down the state before it turned east by the military village of Fort Ransom and then, more curiously, labored back north to enter the expansive valley of an ice age lake, past Fargo east to enter the Red River and fall north toward Hudson Bay. I stared at the leisurely sprawl of its blue line, a finite river beginning in particular, taking its time and space around Dakota, and ending in particular—a little alpha, a little omega, a little territory in between.

That night I promised myself I'd follow this ordinary stream I hadn't greatly noticed in a landscape I took for granted. I would read and study and, next year, discover anything that happened to be along the way, any local truth true in general. North Dakota *was* Everywhere.

I didn't know what towns I'd find present or absent along its banks, what churchyard cemeteries overlooked it with their patient dead and what farms with their patient living. I didn't yet know the geographer who crossed it for the sake of science or the general for the sake of war or where the Cheyenne built the single namesake village. I didn't know what connections I'd find between the present and the past as I tried to follow it, camp beside it, canoe it, fall into it. I didn't know I'd try to sleep in the empty village itself or stand in a child's empty ghost-town bedroom. When I came to Dakota those years ago, I didn't remember my mother was born here, that I had the connection of beginning, and I didn't foresee that my children and their families would end up living here, the connection of staying, or that I'd leave, the connection of departure.

That night, I folded up my map and went to bed. Soon snow would be coming and I relaxed, imagining that anonymous lake at the continental heart turning white in the months to come. And somewhere near that center the little Sheyenne might be starting, following its own directions under a crust of ice in a world I could not, for the moment, imagine.

acknowledgments

Thanks to the following journals for publishing chapters or parts of chapters: *Arkansas Review, Ascent, North Dakota Quarterly, North Dakota Weekly, South Dakota Review,* and *Weber Studies: Voices and Viewpoints of the Contemporary West.*

I also want to acknowledge the help given to me by North Dakotans along the way, including Lester and Eugene who talked of their lives and Frank Beaver and Isaac Schlosser who showed me the insides of rivers. I'm grateful for my colleagues in the University of North Dakota English Department, including William Borden, Robert Lewis, James McKenzie, and Jay Meek. William Kloefkorn closely read the original manuscript and gave helpful advice as did other friends. I also thank all of the writers whose books have helped me see more and understand more about Dakota.

stepping twice
          into the river

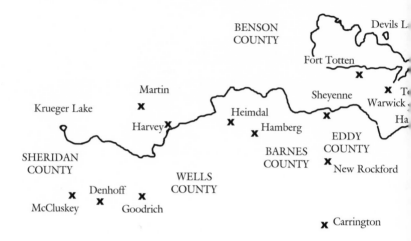

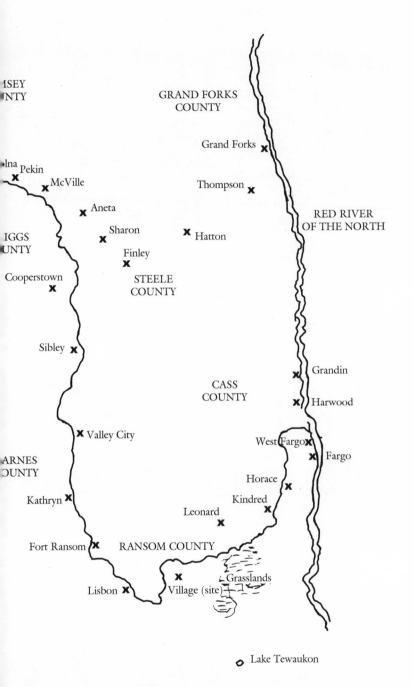

around the beginning in sheridan county

Near the center of Sheridan County, a few miles south of the continental midpoint, I passed a hand-painted sign stuck along the road: "America's Outback." It was cold and gray and the thermos-cup of coffee on the dashboard of the Escort was starting to steam up the glass so I rolled the window down a little, a grit of ice blasting in as I turned onto a gravel road. With the snowmelt flooding every coulee and roadside ditch, every prairie pothole and low field, I was heading upstream to find a river in a world increasingly made of water.

I almost knew where I was going, but it hadn't been easy. A report from the 1900s claimed the river started a few miles from Devils Lake, already two counties behind me, and a 1949 geological pamphlet said Jones Lake, about ten miles behind. Ahead to the north lay a water called Sheyenne Lake, suggesting someone had thought *that* a likely source.

I'd collected maps from the glove compartment, a kitchen drawer, and the gas station down the street. On one, a solid blue line labeled "Sheyenne" came out of Sheyenne Lake. On another, an unnamed line slid upstream from the lake to Highway 14 before breaking into blue dots. The third had a labeled, solid line under Highway 14 and on west and then, finally, north, a little hook of blue in the middle of a blankness. When I found a recent geologic report naming Krueger Lake as the source, even farther north, I'd taken the map that showed the longest blue line.

I rolled up the window against the stinging pellets of rain, turned the windshield wipers on again, and sipped the last of the coffee I'd bought in McClusky, wondering if it would stop raining or rain more or turn to snow, and feeling like one of the last people on earth. Or one of the people on the last of the earth.

I'd always played down the state's remote image as a lazy stereotype that meant nothing except that it seemed far away from whoever said it. A more serious point is how remote it can seem when you're in the middle of it, and that morning something almost eerie lay across the landscape. Steinbeck, traveling with his dog Charley, had reacted with "mysterious responses" to a strange wind in western North Dakota, had said he "felt unwanted in this land," although I only felt irrelevant as I drove, a pair of eyes looking out of my little car at the large land. It was agricultural country—fences along the road, soggy haystacks, the furrows in fields from last fall's plowing—but with no one around, not a house, no machinery working, no seeding yet done, the ground seemed uninhabited, almost original. The dark furrows echoed lines of elevation on a map, each swirl and curve of the plow following the topography of round hills and smooth dips so that the prints of human industry seemed here the design of the earth itself.

And here's how it began: I was driving that day in the middle of the end of what geologists call "an event," the word oddly out of proportion to our practical sense of something you watch happening. Everywhere around me, glaciers had pushed down heavily, thinned, disappeared, come again, repeating for years, for thousands of years. The southern two-thirds of Sheridan County was the Missouri Coteau, hills and sloughs caused by the final collapse of stagnating glaciers with their silt and clay and pebbles. And the northern third, where I was now, the undulating Glaciated Plains shaped by the push of ice and then, at its retreat, by the thick deposits of sediment piled three hundred feet below the thin highway and the surrounding fields. It looked as if the last ice had just melted and one man had driven a tractor across the remnants of earth.

The landscape was monotonous and confusing at the same time. The glaciers' thrust and scour, their dropped loads of sediment, their irregular outwash channels, had made the landscape a complication of forms—stippled and puddled, ridged and hollowed, mounded and cut. The same shapes repeated themselves, elaborating their patterns over the rolling countryside at the same time that they dulled it into a uniform blur. It was not a wilderness, of course, but it seemed a wildness, the relic of an unimaginable "event" that had happened and disappeared and left its mark.

An almost unnerving namelessness surrounded me, although I knew by now there had been names, that in 1900 Charlie Peterson arrived in Sheridan County from Sweden and Anton Peterson from Denmark. John Janson and Martin Melvold came from Norway and John Mutschler came from Russia as did John Winter and Gottlieb Diede, Freadrich Sauter and Freadrich Jenner, Pauline Enders and Johanna Schock and Margaret Frey. Not all stayed—or even most—and of those who did many of their children or grandchildren didn't, but some mailboxes still carry the names of homesteaders.

North Dakota's population slipped by 2 percent or so in the early 1990s, one of the few states to have that happen, but Sheridan County declined by almost a quarter in that time, and almost three-quarters since 1910, a date of notable departures I'd come upon again and again. That year, Dakota swelled to approximately 600,000, some counties falling off immediately, the whole state's population peaking in the 1930s. Now about 42,000 fewer citizens are gathered around the heart of the continent than in 1910, the year Sheridan County averaged about eight per square mile.

Of the twenty-four post-office stations listed in Sheridan County's history, I'd found six and the highway map listed four, the truth of history both natural and human, advance and retreat, the sound our voices make in the air before drifting away.

Let's, for a moment, follow the arithmetic of those twenty-four names. Some called a halfway point on a military trail Bass Station, some called it Middle Station, but there was no need to call it anything when the Northern Pacific ended the need for trails. Take away Berlin's rural post office operating only half of 1889 and Tiebell and Wehr, rescinded even before they started. Then subtract the farm post offices soon made unnecessary, Wittmayer and Schmidt, closed by 1902, and Curtis and Herr, closed by 1912.

Take away Dudley and take away Clark, which combined to become Goodrich, and forget Blaine which someone thought was the new name of Goodrich for nine days before it was rescinded. Cross out Pickardsville because people misspelled it so frequently as Pickardville that it was changed after the first six months and don't count Casselman, the old name for Martin, or Lincoln, the old name for Lincoln Valley. Don't count Old McClusky after the new McClusky moved three miles east to be on the Northern Pacific tracks and don't count Lamont because it disappeared after it lost the county seat to McClusky. Of Skogmo, take heed. A rural community from the early 1890s, post office closed in 1932, last store burned in 1940, Skogmo now lay as a plowed field, seeds of wheat in the ashes of old stores, streets buried beneath the furrows.

Such subtraction left six names. One was the ghost town of Lincoln Valley and I shrugged that off, not imagining I would return at the last of the summer's journey to actually find it and stand in the ruins of a child's house. The second was Martin—settled by Rumanians in 1896, home to two hundred people in the '40s, but only half that now—where I'd accidentally stopped last year, not wondering about the Sheyenne. I had a solitary beer at the Somewhere Else Lounge, then went across the street to J&W Upholstery, the only commercial enterprise visible except for the elevator and some snowmobiles lined up in a front yard. The owner at J&W mainly did canvas repair, tarps, rain covers for farm equipment, that kind of thing. Oh, he was from here, all right. His grandparents had homesteaded forty miles south—he nodded in that direction—and he was born there. Next year was the Martin Centennial. "We'll do something for it," he said. Pause. "I imagine."

Today, coming west across the bottom of the county on Highway 200, I'd visited the other four names, Northern Pacific towns established a few minutes into the twentieth century. I'd driven through Goodrich thinking about Doug Wick's story from 1901, his *North Dakota Place Names* beside me on the seat. James Clark platted five blocks for the town of Clark, the main street being Clark Avenue, and a Mr. Dudley platted a rival town site halfway around it, calling it—well, calling it Dudley. "After a few good rounds of country politics," as Wick says, the two were combined and called Goodrich for the Northern Pacific civil engineer in charge of local construction.

Sometimes we called places for people who helped build them—Mr. Goodrich, Mr. Fargo, Mr. Dickinson—and some for where they were or what was around—Valley City, Grand Forks—and some for places we came from, names you could trace upstream. Denhoff, the next town on Highway 200, was named for the postmaster's former home, Alt-Donhoff, in South Russia, but Alt-Donhoff, of course, is not Russian. Germans moving into the Russian area of Cololobowka brought along the name of Count Donhoff of Berlin, people carrying their past with them across this central plain and for a century.

Denhoff peaked in 1920 with 323 residents, its population no longer reported. County historians said it was a Wild West town before the railroad reached it, known for its "blind-piggers" and their supply of liquor. Patrons living along the trail could spot the sheriff heading to town and usually beat him there so all the liquor would be hidden, everything peaceful, when he arrived. When I arrived, everything still seemed peaceful, no one on the street, and I drove on, the ditches swelling with icy water, the surrounding fields dark and open and waiting.

Wanting to refill my thermos I turned toward McClusky— Mr. McClusky a pioneer settler from Nebraska—driving now on 700 feet of glacial till and slowing at a sign proclaiming it the geographical center of North Dakota, a point of pride I decided not to question. The stores still open on main street survived inside the brutal architecture of the steel shed but they carried the hope of familiar names: SuperValu Grocery, Rexall Drug, Hardware Hank, Farmer's Union Oil Company. Most of the closed-up stores—McClusky now only half of its 1940s population of 924—had rustic false-fronts, which gave off a western feel, halfway between the 100th and 101st meridians, a frontier at one time and now, apparently, another.

I parked and thought about going into Helm's Tavern—"For Sale by Owner"—but it was only ten o'clock so I chose coffee and went into the cafe next door, a decision without a difference as the two were connected inside. With half a dozen people in the bar and no one else in the cafe, I asked for a thermos fill-up and a cup to go. A poster on the wall noted that the price for wheat represented eight cents for each dollar of the finished product. In *The McClusky Gazette* on the table, editor Jim Wills supported the Supreme Court's decision overturning a law against firearms within one thousand feet of a school because that meant everybody living within three blocks of the McClusky school, a good number of townsfolk, "myself included," said Editor Wills, would have to walk around to go duck hunting at Lake Lilly.

Pickardville, a few more miles west and no longer named on the highway map, was a quick tour. Mr. Pickard, said to be the only Civil War veteran pioneer in North Dakota, had served under Sherman on the March to the Sea, then marched here to start a new life with his brother-in-law as postmaster. But Pickard's town never really developed—there was a fluke high of twenty-three people in 1960—and all I had to do was turn off the highway one block, drive past a few houses and the elevator, and I was back on the highway again, completing my tour of the towns of Sheridan County.

I'd finished the last of the McClusky coffee when I came to the sign for Sheyenne Lake, so I left the asphalt for an unpaved road, winding through the same undulating glacial plains but here, as a wildlife refuge, with more natural cover. The road got soggier and my tires were starting to spin a little in the loose sandy tracks so that, when I came over a small hill and pointed down toward a catastrophe, I had to pump the brakes cautiously to stop.

The road below, a causeway between two lakes, disappeared under a rush of water for twenty or thirty yards and then emerged. Such waters, even a few inches deep, often ate away at roads while hiding the danger and I wasn't going to risk it. I got out, zipped my jacket, and walked down. The rushing surge impressed me but nothing around suggested it was unusual. The trees, the land, the road—everything—accepted this small spring disaster with complete equanimity, the waters gurgling almost cheerfully as they poured over the downstream edge of the road. I couldn't tell if this was a flooded Sheyenne Lake, its sister Coal Mine Lake, the Sheyenne River, or the merging of all of them.

I stood in a world of cold earth, water, and air, feeling at least a twinge of what it was like to live completely dependent on those elements, before railroads, before towns. With few trees for lumber, settlers sometimes dug their first home into the earth itself—a pithouse or tunnel into a hillside—or built it out of the earth, piling rocks and sod, or firing bricks of clayey soil. Many found soft lignite coal buried beneath their feet, hundreds of farmers and ranchers digging their own. They cut ice in winter and gathered buffalo bones in summer, often a first source of cash, and the first year planted potatoes—those mealy white chunks of earth and water—and wheat after that and wheat again, pioneers soon calling the territory after the grain, "Land of the No. 1 Hard."

They dug at the earth, wrenching up rocks left by millennial glaciers, lugging them on wooden stone-boats to a pile, hundreds of these monuments to hardship now dotting the fields. Add to this the weather, the surly summer heating the wheat to the yellow-white blaze of the sun, autumn stripping the landscape into a different color of monotony, the winter's snow blowing over empty fields and rocks and bones, making everything seem even more the same almost unendurably and then, every spring, water again, melting from the snow, filling the coulees, welling up in the fields, pushing and urging. It was a life lived not simply on the earth, but from deep within it.

I turned away from the mild gushing flood, walked back to my car, and retraced the mile or so of sandy road. On the highway again, I drove north to the bridge over what my map called the Sheyenne and walked to the middle, leaning against the concrete wall and looking west at another version of landscape. The furrows of agriculture still aligned themselves with the glacial topography of swell and hollow but now they found an echo in the multiple small waters moving in curves and crescents and whirls through a marshy indecision before, I realized, they were artificially channeled beneath me, a highway needing to cross a sprawling wetland, dozens of dark spring seeps made into a decisive stream by engineers.

I leaned against the bridge wall until the cold seeping into my thighs from the concrete became too much and retreated to the Escort, sitting for a moment and bending my face to the heater's dusty air, rubbing my hands in front of the panel vents. Taking one last look out the window, I started off toward the county road that would take me west toward Krueger Lake, a blue circle in the map's white space, no named road near it.

I'd read enough to uncover one mystery: the Sheyenne's curious course through the state. Wherever it began, it soon only followed an ancient trench gouged by catastrophe. As the ice age climate warmed, glaciers melted and rainfall increased sending floods through lakes and spillways from Saskatchewan down across Dakota in almost unimaginably gigantic surges. In the 1997 Grand Forks flood, which swamped half the town after I left, the Red River carried something like a hundred thousand cubic feet of water per second, leaving humans helpless. The ice age floods brought three million cubic feet per second down the countryside, a huge valley-digging flow gushing south, east, south again, sliding briefly up a lift of land to surrender and pour back northeasterly, emptying into glacial Lake Agassiz. The Sheyenne is, therefore, an "underfit stream" in scientific terms, winding inside a valley not of its making, something present inside something absent.

Different assumed sources for the river explained the discrepancies in how long it lasted in North Dakota—325 miles in one book, 550 in a geology pamphlet, in the dictionary at 523—but there was another answer. Although the ditches swelled full today on both sides of the road and a surge of water by some name ate away at the road to Sheyenne Lake, one source called the river "ephemeral" and another "intermittent" in its upper regions, the reason for dotted blue lines on a map. *Where* the Sheyenne starts has to do with *when* it starts, here one season, there another. In the uncertain earth around me I searched for a river following an ice age course, underfit and intermittent.

The wind was stronger now, whipping droplets of rain against the windshield, and I came to an intersection, a farmhouse and a few outbuildings on one corner. A man heading inside stopped to watch as a stranger's car slowed. Here were my directions, I thought, and turned into his driveway, stopped, and got out.

"Just doin' some mud work," he said when I came up, answering a question I hadn't thought of.

"I'm trying to find Krueger Lake," I said.

"What's your name?" he asked, gruffly, I thought, but I told him.

"Koenig?" He leaned forward and cupped his hand behind his ear.

"King." I tried to enunciate the single syllable in the icy wind between us, but I wanted to let it go at "Koenig" because that's what it would be if I were German Russian, the largest national group in Sheridan County to which belonged, I assumed, Mr. Krueger of Krueger Lake and the Dakota citizen I faced now.

After getting my last name he went after the first and I felt a slight flare of impatience, but I was the stranger coming into his territory so I slowed down. Maybe in a landscape with few people, it was important to know who each one was, especially with a license plate from East Dakota. I told him my names, received his, and nodded.

"German Russian, then?" I asked.

Oh, yes. His grandparents came from the Black Sea area. They were Rumanians. "Well, you know," he said, shrugging, "The Black Sea was under Russia, Germany, Turkey. So some of those early guys wrote down they were born in Turkey and some in Austria and some in Rumania." He grinned. "And they were all born in pretty much the same place."

When Russia went back on its promise of military exemption for German farmers settling the Black Sea area, they'd started coming here in the 1870s, some going first to South Dakota but, with less free land there by that time, then moved on north. In the 1880s—the Great Dakota Boom—people "flooded in," the usual phrase, a rush of rapid settlement, which built up North Dakota's

German Russian triangle, its base six counties along the southern border, its apex two in the north. Up there most of the neighbors were from six German Catholic villages near Odessa; here the Sheyenne ran through 95 percent German Protestant country.

They were the only major group of immigrants from a semi-arid country so they knew about living on a treeless plain, but after the prairie was broken up and the topsoil began to blow away traditional farming methods proved difficult. Many German Russians went on to Canada but a lot stayed, proving difficult enough themselves and described by others as frugal or practical, tough-minded or simply rough, but surely hard-working. The men abused themselves and their wives and children with work, doing without, and then doing without some more. Single-mindedly, almost crude-mindedly in the eyes of their sometimes scandalized neighbors, they lived in primitive conditions and worked their farms and saved their money to buy another farm, when it was up for sale, and then another. The very phrase "mud work" was a present echo of the unforgiving heaviness of such labor in the past—Land of the Number One Hard in more than one way.

I asked my question again and he waved ahead. "Just straight on west the way you're heading. Road turns north at the lake."

"It's the headwaters of the Sheyenne," I explained to the man who lived a mile from it. "I'm trying to find where it starts."

"Well," he nodded and paused. "That could be."

"It's not the headwaters?" I asked.

"Oh, yeah, could be," he shrugged. "Only sometimes water drains north from here. In the fifties, one year? There was a lot of rain around and you could see all them lakes empty northward. Of course," he relented, "that could've been unusual, you know."

"Well, I don't know myself," I said, knowing my turn to back down when I heard it. "But thanks. Appreciate it."

When I came to where the road turned north by a farmhouse, nothing ahead but two muddy tracks along the fence and the hazy tip of a dark body of water beyond it, I pulled into the driveway and knocked to ask permission. No one answered, so I parked at a tilt on the road and walked up the soggy field path, squinting against the icy spit, half snow by now. At my feet ran thick ribbons of earth, the rounded tops of burrows dug under the snow in winter by pocket gophers, I imagined, and now on top of something rather than beneath it, one season's secrets turned to another's momentary wreckage. Then I turned off the path, stepping gingerly across the spongy snow-matted grass until I was at the water's edge.

To my right lay the lake, hills holding it in to the west, a pebbly gray shore on this side, dark water lifting in front of me out of its source, a minor flood curling through marsh grass and cattails, then around a stranded roll of hay. If the Sheyenne began ten thousand years ago in a natural catastrophe, it was beginning again today, half winter, half spring, right out there somewhere.

I was aware of being very alone and very much out of my personal time. Glaciers moved laboriously down for eons, then melted away slowly or in flood, names of pioneers streaming across the land, some streaming away again and, in front of me, eddies roiled and rippled without purpose or with implacable purpose. Finally, I saw it, I'm sure I saw it, a certain insistence in the flow, a current marked by flecks of foam that moved more quickly than others, swirling one way and another but moving on, indicating a future. This was it—alone, I still nodded to myself—all this water "born pretty much in the same place" regardless of names, a beginning that seemed chaotic but was only a natural rhythm repeating and multiplying. This didn't feel like the Out Back, after all, but like the Deep Within, some secret I couldn't translate even to myself, ignorant as water but familiar with its feel. I stood for a few more minutes at the beginning of everything moving away into what was to come and, after another long gaze out into the current, trudged back across the grass, slipping a few times on the wet hummocks, following the muddy lane back to the car.

Then, one other thing. I took a different county road back toward the highway and in a mile suddenly had to stop. In front of me a rivulet from the flooded ditch had incised a one-foot-deep, one-foot-wide canyon straight across the gravel road. I got out to inspect it, looking down on a tiny rippling river, already sorting its stones, sand at the bottom, then gravel, then pebbles lined up as in any stream. An overnight accident, it could have been here for years, water always acting exactly this way. I stood and watched it follow its nature while interrupting ours, then got in the car and turned, backed, turned, backed, and drove away, my wheel marks on the wet sand of the shoulder showing the exact design of my reversal.

continental divide: looking back across the years

"I always remember saying goodbye," my mother said of her years spent traveling between her father's Montana homestead and her older sister's North Dakota town. "You'd think I'd remember arriving, but I only remember leaving."

And once in the Rockies my father pointed to a ridge high above his very young son. If I poured a cup of water there, one half would leave for the Pacific, the other half for the Atlantic. I demanded we climb and try it, but he needed to drive on. "Theoretically," I think he said.

That morning, a month after watching one river rise from many waters, I drove Highway 52 toward Harvey, the first town in Wells County to receive the Sheyenne. With the bright May sun hitting the windshield and making it warmer in the car than it made the spring earth outside, I was arriving at an unlikely Continental Divide, a subtle height of land that pushed the Sheyenne to the Red and north to Hudson Bay while the James—through the Missouri and Mississippi—emptied southward into the Gulf. Both ended in the Atlantic so it wasn't a "true" divide, a geologist friend had sniffed, but it seemed enough to look for. Thus I was heading toward the division of a dotted line, the James behind, the Sheyenne ahead, less than ten miles apart, the difference in elevation about six feet.

A 1929 history of Wells County philosophized that these two rivers, rising side by side to separate and leave, were "emblematic of the course pursued by many families of the human race," a phrase echoing the rhythms of migrations across the old continents, across oceans to this land, across this land to here, first leaving and arriving, then staying or leaving again.

In 1917, James Boyle, a field agent at the Experimental Station in Fargo, drove for thirty days across the state, discovering departures—in one county, for example, four-fifths of the homesteaders had quit in twenty years. But Boyle complained the abandoned sod houses dotting the countryside gave a false impression. The land of those leaving had been bought by those staying, one section with three original settlers gone but the fourth now with their land, a new house and barn, and nearby another pioneer held the fields of six departing neighbors, some leaving but some—absolutely—staying.

The *1970 Wells County Centennial History* put the pioneer experience—and a present reaction—into two poignant sentences:

"As we look back across the years, we are reminded of the high hopes, the stunning disappointments and the heroic struggles the pioneers endured. We realize that every foot of soil is hallowed with tears and toil and prayers."

It was difficult, driving with huge open fields on either side, to imagine the landscape divided into feet of soil, and also difficult to think of it as anything but solid, the white farmhouses every few miles as anything but permanent. Nevertheless, this had always been a landscape for journeys.

Our human time here began as Stone-Age bands hunted the edges of glaciers. Or it began as The People slowly gathered— Assiniboine, Cree, Yankton, Mandan, Hidatsa, and Arikara. Or as Red River buffalo hunters rode west or Missouri River trappers moved east or Hudson Bay Company hunters came south. Or it began—and this is our favorite way because we love the sound of our own names and numbers—with the Stevens Expedition in 1853.

Surveying a railroad route to the Pacific, Stevens came up near what would be, and then scarcely be, Wellsburgh to the Sheyenne's "high banks and no wood," easily crossed its south fork, forty feet wide and two deep with a gravely bottom, and went on. Ten years later, on a journey of gold, Captain Fisk's wagon train headed to Montana through northern Wells followed by journeys of war, Sibley's expedition against the Sioux in 1863 and, two years later, Sully moving toward Devils Lake, fording the Sheyenne near Harvey.

On its own journey, the Sheyenne curled into Wells County along Pony Gulch, its hill a mile-long glacial end moraine, its valley a condensed history. Buffalo once grazed by a nearby lake and moved on, The People who hunted them leaving stone tipi-rings, a round memory, and the lake drying into prairie air, another round memory, its bottom furrowed into farmland. Plows still cut across old campsites, blading up beads and flint and arrowheads.

Scotch Bill, an early trapper, came and went, giving the gulch its name by getting caught in a late winter blizzard in the 1870s, digging into the moraine for shelter and killing his pony for food, sitting it out until spring break-up. A few years later, settlers journeyed toward Pony Gulch to Ivey's Lignite Coal Mine, a pit dug to reach the coal fifteen feet beneath the prairie. Barbara Levorsen, a Wells County child then, remembered her father taking a three-day wagon ride in winter to get there, shoveling away at the almost exhausted layer of lignite, and getting back home. Remembered her mother being lonely, remembered "Father said he was very tired when he got home that evening."

But the Pony Gulch story I'd never forget came from the 1880s when John Coff got badly frozen in a blizzard. After weeks of suffering he died from having his feet amputated, Mrs. Coff then becoming, by poison, the county's first suicide. In the mid-1920s a Soo Line steam shovel exposed some bones near Harvey, and an old pioneer claimed they were the remains of Mrs. Coff. She'd been buried in that "pretty spot" along the Sheyenne, he remembered, another piece of Wells County earth, after great pain from without and great pain within, hallowed by tears and toil and prayers.

I drove beside the Soo Line—trying to imagine what it felt like to see, or hope to see, the twin lifelines of tracks crossing the otherwise blank prairie in the 1890s and hooking Harvey to Manfred to Fessenden to Emrick to Cathay. Part of my family arrived by railroad as well, although it took me a long time to find this out.

Montana had provided the main early stories but when I moved to Grand Forks my mother reminded me she'd lived there, she'd been *born* in North Dakota, a fact I'd so firmly forgotten I insisted she'd never told me.

A few years ago, her sister's son Bill researched and wrote *The Johnsons of North Dakota,* which recounts the trip, turn of the century, of my grandfather Charlie with wife Lottie and daughter Esther, to North Dakota. And what a move it was. They rented a boxcar for their belongings and, families being permitted to accompany their goods, Charlie and Esther went along, lunches tucked in dresser drawers, boxes and trunks jiggling in rhythm to the tracks. Father and daughter sat on two rocking chairs, the broad doors open, the northern landscape unscrolling itself in front of them. "One continuous picnic," Bill writes, his mother's childhood recollection.

Charlie arrived in North Dakota's Richburg—we named parts of the land for our desires—and partnered with the postmaster, Jules Beaudoin, to run the Pioneer Store. When the Great Northern tracks were laid two miles west of town a year later, the Johnsons, with almost everyone else and a substantial portion of Richburg's buildings, moved to the new site, the Great Northern's slogan "Hope of the West" condensed into my mother's 1907 birthplace—Westhope. When she told me, I could barely believe it. West Hope.

Many journeys in Dakota show the mix of its citizens. To the west, the Sheyenne was a German Russian river, to the east, Norwegian, and the town names suggested uneasy neighbors. Heimdal honored the Norse guardian of the rainbow bridge and Bremen its German original. Viking was Viking from 1911 to 1913 when the majority German population renamed it Hamberg. In Wells, the townships of Germantown, Hamburg, and Bremen are just south of Valhalla and Norway Lake.

Looking back, it's easy to think the northern plains blended their immigrant nations into a happily democratic family. The name Jules Beaudoin echoes another country, and my aunt Esther would soon marry Paulo Conte, the Italian-born music professor newly arrived in Grand Forks, so it seemed those who had arrived were busily becoming Americans. Dakota novelist Larry Woiwode believes the ethnic and religious conflicts of the pioneer experience, together with common tragedies, helped knit communities together. "Often, in the smallest community," he writes, "you have acceptance of a multiplicity of diversity" and he looks back on his own family settling along the Rice River while the Sioux still traveled between Canada and South Dakota, his great-grandmother's farm one of the watering places on the way.

But it is also easy to find conflict as different arrivals collided. A few counties west, in Wilton, the Anglo Saxon Presbyterians ran the businesses, Swedes farmed to the south, and Ukrainians occupied the homesteads north in "Snake Town," the trains taking miners to the nearby coal fields dubbed Garlic Specials. Last week in a small town cafe I heard a Norwegian farmer shake his head and remark, "Well, I only know one other Swede and he doesn't like me either." A few years ago I asked a North Dakota history professor what part of Grand Forks he grew up in. He glanced at me for a long second. "They called it Jew Town," he replied.

In Rolvaag's *Their Fathers' God*, Beret, the fated wife of immigrant Per Hansa, is told of a Norwegian Lutheran neighbor marrying an Irish Catholic and she immediately thinks of the Biblical distinction between the sons of God, her own, and the daughters of men. "Out here," she thinks, "people seemed no longer to care with whom they mixed and whored."

Not yet American, we staked out pieces of landscape. "Nothing but Indians and foreigners up there," a friend tells Per Hansa's son of Bismarck. And in Wells County, Barbara Levorsen remembered ill feelings between the immigrant settlers and the English-speaking, store-owning Yankees who took advantage of them. Roosians and Norskies, citizens of Hamburg and Viking, we came together and stayed apart, each homestead, for better and for worse, a journey over long distance and an arrival.

I was by now halfway between Manfred and Harvey, the Continental Divide somewhere near, a river turning south behind me, a river turning north ahead. I pulled onto a field road over a culvert and got out, camera in hand, searching the landscape for any change of elevation in the slight rises and swales around me. A pickup went by, the driver nodding and then looking around himself, puzzling at what I'd found to take a picture of.

Bristles of last year's grass stuck out beneath my shoes as I stood about 1,600 feet above sea level and, considering time, on the thinnest of surfaces. Looking back across the years also meant looking down into the darkness below my feet. I remembered an illustration in James Hutton's 1795 *Theory of the Earth*—the beginning of modern geology—that showed the cutaway view of a Scottish riverbank. At the bottom, triangles of metamorphic rock thrust up, covered by pebbles covered by layers of sediment and then some bushes, a tree, a fence, one gentleman on horseback greeting a carriage. It was slightly unnerving, these eighteenth-century humans hailing each other on the top of eons, but it is how we live, whether we remember it or not, at each step of our way.

And to imagine that journey, 1915 was an important year, around here the time Saundersville was platted a few miles the other side of Harvey, a bustling little town, some old-timers recalled, although in ten years it was legally dissolved, its name sometimes drifting up to the surface in a county atlas. But 1915 was also the year of Alfred Wegener's *The Origin of Continents and Oceans*, proposing our beginning in a single landmass, Pangaea, "all earth," which divided into a cosmic couple, Gondwana to the south and Laurasia to the north, soon to multiply and divide. The earth's crust, we know now, is a series of moving plates, the ground under our feet on its own travels, if excruciatingly slow, the speed our fingernails grow. I stood in one place that afternoon but the place had not been standing in one place. Thus, as with the Sheyenne's headwaters, the *where* is ultimately a matter of the *when*.

Thinking of our history in "deep time," as John McPhee calls that unthinkable ache of calculation, we grow weary with its murmuring repetitions of "millions of years ago," so we've abbreviated that massive stretch to *mya*. Let us say, then, five hundred mya, a chunk of North America floated, the equator across the little imaginary rectangle of North Dakota, Harvey a sandy seabottom, Grand Forks a lowland slowly being eaten away by the waves. Four hundred mya, we rose above sea level for a collision with the fragment of James Hutton's Scotland which sent the rivers of Dakota flowing west, and forty million later the seas flooded in again, compressing plant and animal life to form more than half of the state's oil and gas resources.

At three hundred and twenty mya, masses of land came together again, Wells County's Cathay and China's Ch'in pressed close for eighty million years until another breakup, shallow waves rippling over a sandy bottom to the west, a muddy plain to the east. For millions of years, we were a moist lowland forest, for millions more another sea bottom, sand and mud over Richburg, over Westhope. Eroded in dry climates and built up in wet, Dakota rose and fell as if the world were breathing in a long sleep.

One hundred mya, drifting well north of the equator, Wells County was the muddy bottom of a central waterway stretching to Texas, Idaho a western upland, Wisconsin an eastern shore. North America now in its familiar position, the rising Rockies cut off the flow of moist air from the Pacific, insuring Norway Lake and Germantown together a continental climate of hot summers and cold winters.

More catastrophes followed from the west, uplifts and erosions and volcanoes, surging rivers carrying dirt and volcanic ash—*detritus,* Latin for "worn away"—as they wound through swamps, adding layers of silt and clay, of matted leaves and rotting wood from trees twelve feet wide, a hundred feet tall. About sixty mya, the seas swelled inland again, their weight pressing down to form North Dakota's coal, the lignite beds of Ivey's Mine, the coal that John Coff, freezing, wished he had.

Fifty, then twenty mya, North Dakota was almost at its present latitude and almost tropical—palms under Manfred, corals under Harvey—and the pulses continued, ages of accumulation and removal. The backward clock at two mya, glaciers ground forward and retreated, melting into new rivers emptying northward, then, five hundred thousand years later, southward. "Water just wants to find the easiest way," my father once explained, but how torturous the easy way could be, the landscape a slow chaos of repetitive change, the earth itself arriving, earth departing.

The last glacier down buried most of North Dakota under several thousand feet of ice and, after another eternity, retreated, the age of the catastrophic floods, which the Sheyenne and James now followed, dwarfed in their broad valleys. For three thousand years, stagnant ice lingered below hundreds of feet of glacial outwash, dense spruce forests growing in earth on top of the ice on top of the earth. Warmer and drier eight thousand years ago, it turned cool and moist five thousand years ago, changed for a thousand, changed for a thousand, cool and moist this age, this late May morning.

I stood a few yards off Highway 52 in Wells County in the Holocene Age, the recent time of 11,000 years ago, the camera in my hand set to an exposure of $1/125$ of a second. Beside me was a brown field and, across the road, a white farmhouse, the sky a purity of spring blue. I looked for something in the countryside with enough lift to separate two rivers and send them off, like the migrations of families, but I couldn't find it. I took a photograph in each of the four directions, as if I were offering a prayer to the winds, then slid back in the driver's seat and started off. Later, I couldn't distinguish them from any others I'd taken that morning, too many other white houses, blue skies, too many brown fields.

I came into Harvey, the radio blasting messages from businesses to graduating seniors, and parked in front of a building, "Restaurant" painted on the window although a large Rexall sign hung above the door. It turned out to be a new cafe replacing the drugstore and I took a seat along the wall under a sign that promised "Food So Good You'd Think Your Grandma Was in the Kitchen," trying to decide between the Spaghetti Dinner with Salad and the

Hot Beef or Hot Hamburger Sandwich with Gravy. The waitress headed over, pausing to admonish a somber farmer bending over his spaghetti, "Come on! How can you not smile when the sun's finally shining?" I ordered a Hot Beef Sandwich out of habit, then asked about the new business. She was a co-owner, as it turned out, one of two women, and business was good—well, right now it was slow, of course, planting, all the farmers out in the fields most of the time. But it seemed busy enough to me and I ate, watching older couples having lunch, four middle-aged women chatting together along the wall, a mother and her daughter and the daughter's child in front of me.

Leaving, I stopped by the door to look through the North Central phone book, which listed three other towns: Rugby, that old continental center; Bottineau, where my grandfather Charlie's brother had a store in 1906; and Minot, where one of my daughters lived after marrying another North Dakotan who wasn't born here, a big part of their lives determined by where their parents journeyed. In the Yellow Pages, I counted one aircraft service and one funeral home, two furniture stores, three banks, four restaurants (including the Tastee Freeze), five law firms, and eight churches. Down 10 percent in the last decade, Harvey's population had still managed to stay over 2,000 since mid-century, no small task for a small town in the northern plains.

I put back the phone book and stepped into the midday light of the industrious town. Citizens came to lunch and left, pickups lumbered by with trailers of anhydrous ammonia and, as the woman had said, come on, the sun was shining. Standing in a territory called North Central, I was both at a distance and at a middle, two newspapers in the red metal racks beside me, one from Bismarck a hundred miles southwest, one from Minot a hundred miles northwest. I drove south, past the Town and Country Supper Club and

Bowling Lanes and was suddenly, thoughtlessly, beside the Sheyenne itself.

To the west, enlarged behind a dam, loomed something like a lake although, curving between small hills, it had the feel of a river. I pulled over, getting out to look across the calm water and then down at the small culvert through which it disappeared. Dodging pickups, I crossed the road and found the little trickle of the Sheyenne lapping beneath a railroad trestle. In 1892, the Soo Line dammed the river to use its waters for locomotives and round-house work, so this was nothing new. I was probably looking directly at the absence of the first store in Harvey, 1893, a large tent on the north bank just south of the Soo tracks.

I headed back north to find the river and, the road rising out of town, came upon another surprise. Below me, the Sheyenne, no more than three feet wide, curled tamely through the lawn of the Harvey golf course. We've done much worse to American rivers than fill steam-locomotives with them or trim them into pastoral golf-course streams, but I was disappointed for a moment, so reduced did it seem, so owned. Still, it wound where it had to go, here and always leaving.

In a mile or so, the Sheyenne curved north and I helplessly followed the straight highway into miles of open countryside, the sky clouding over, the land a forlorn gray. Ahead, a tractor moved toward me in a field so large it took a long time for us to meet, no time at all to pass, the farmer waving as I waved. Business was going on here, but done by one man at a time, and although it was owned or rented, no longer prairie, the land seemed even wider as I drove on, dwarfing my car as it had done the tractor.

I had a few glimpses of my own pioneer family because Bill had sent some homestead photographs he'd found. In one, Grampa Charlie stands in baggy coat and pants by the side of the house awkwardly holding out a brace of rabbits in each hand, squinting from under his cap against the sunlight, his flat field behind him. There was also one of my mother—a child in white dress, long stockings, a round white hat sending a shadow over her face—standing on a gigantic boulder ice-hauled from Canada a couple of millennia ago. "Olson" was painted in white cursive, nothing around her but the short-grass prairie, despite that claim of ownership.

It is difficult to describe this "bleak and barren country," as Eric Sevareid remembered it, "where the skyline offered nothing to soothe the senses," but everyone through here has tried. *Giants in the Earth* begins with a small caravan plodding "into a bluish-green infinity—on and on, and always farther on." It was hard, Rolvaag wrote, "for the eye to wander from sky line to sky line, year in and year out, without finding a resting place." In 1882, nine-year-old Willa Cather arrived on the Nebraska plains, feeling "as if we had come to the end of everything—it was a kind of erasure of personality."

My mother had a child's memory of the expanse, spring pasqueflowers so numerous they seemed like lakes in the small swales and coulees. And for North Dakota writer Lois Phelps Hudson, growing up in the 1920s, the prairie provided an almost mystical experience. A child who walks "in the loneliness of great spaces," she thought, "absorbs familiarity with eternity" and she felt she herself might have existed for centuries, grass whispering at the shoulders of dreamy buffalo, a plenitude surrounding her.

But the depression and drought of the 1930s arrived and Hudson's family departed. Looking back, she thought there had been a mismatch, the farmer's soul "too small to cherish the immense heritage." She remembered her father grinding his teeth at "the impossible combination of men and elements he faced—the illiterate 'Roosians,' the exploiting farmers, their exploiting absentee landlords, the wind, the drought," and she felt there was something impossibly unbalanced between the individual man and the prairie. "Only nomads," she wrote, "can live in the wastelands of sea, sand, mud, ice, and dust, where the figures of men are forever out of scale."

I drove past fields, most of their promises now planted and waiting, but I also drove through eons, rising and falling seas, rising and falling earths, empty for millennia, crossed by nomads for centuries, settled by the People for centuries more. And then those arrived who brought a certain kind of civilization, not completely harmonious with the past of the prairie, not quite one with its future.

From Richburg to Westhope and on into the West, Charlie Johnson moved, setting forth to lose three farms in his lifetime, beginning with those 640 acres in eastern Montana that Esther remembered for its bad crops, water so alkaline it couldn't be used on the garden, and bugs and mosquitoes so thick you needed netting for any outside work. The summer of 1913, Charlie was out on the homestead, building a house and barn while Lottie sat on a pile of rocks cleared from the dusty fields and wept, miles from the Hope of the West. "No wonder my mother was always crying," my own mother said after a final trip back to that landscape. That fall, Grandmother Lottie died and, in less than a year, Charlie established a legacy of family gossip by marrying their seamstress, Ethel, finally moving onto the homestead my mother called the Highline.

Charlie tried to bring a certain civilization west. To please his musical daughter Esther, he purchased a reed organ, which stood that summer in a tent beside the Montana house, but it ultimately wasn't enough. Her mother's death, his quick re-marriage, and the fact of the bleak homestead itself—"I couldn't take it," Esther later said. She left for North Dakota again, taking my young mother with her, beginning those back and forth years between house and homestead, the train trips of which my mother remembered only saying good-bye although the wheels moved to the rhythm of the chant she later taught me: "Clickety-clack, clickety-clack. Take you there and take you back."

Civilization arrived in Wells County, according to the centennial history, in exactly 1882 with the first social dance and the killing of the county's last buffalo, two more ways to measure arrival and departure. That year—when Cather came to the end of everything on the Nebraska plains—was thus the beginning of one order and the end of another, the year Jesse James was shot, one year after Billy the Kid met the same fate. Charlie Johnson was twelve then and when he turned twenty-three—the homestead barn still twenty years in the future, the last buffalo in Wells County dead for a decade—historian Frederick Turner would proclaim the importance of the frontier to the American character. He would also announce it was closed.

But, for the moment, here they came, settlers and speculators streaming in under the Homestead Act or the Pre-Emption Act or the Timber Culture Act, 160 acres if you planted ten of them to trees. Some worked hard for those trees, like Martin Bohnet over in Germantown Township who, during a drought summer, walked a mile every day to the James, filled his buckets, and walked a mile back. But once you'd proved up with the right number of trees, you could simply plow them under again. The Timber Culture and Pre-Emption Acts were repealed in 1891, the year nearby Fessenden's wheat crop was so large it couldn't be harvested, the farmers too poor to buy threshing machines, the manufacturers and bankers too wary to trust them, everyone exploiting, everyone exploited.

Barbara Levorsen looks back to find some pioneers "followed by misfortune," others "lucky in whatever they undertook," a strange and disheartening aspect of life at these continental extremes. When I thought of heroic struggle and stunning disappointments I thought of the Nehers and the Martins, the story told by daughter and niece Pauline, relayed by Elizabeth Hampsten in *Far From Home*.

Poor German Russian Protestants, the two families arrived in North Dakota, 1909, too late to plant, spending the winter—four adults and seven children—in a boxcar, using dried cow manure mixed with weeds and twigs for fuel, "a winter of confusion," Hampsten writes, the rough men trying to control their fears through frequent and aimless violence in the name of discipline.

The next year they crowded into an abandoned house and began to work their way out of that horror, but only slowly, too short of cash, knowing too little about the weather and soil, their neighbors suspicious or plainly despising them. Even the "true Germans," those not from Russia, suggested buying land as far from their own as possible. Looking back, Pauline's father and uncle said they'd rather forget those terrible first winters, and she remembered it in German. *Diese waren verachte Zeite*—those were desperate times. *Verachte Zeite*.

Shadow surrounded many of the Little Houses on the Prairie, requirements for residence on claims often scattering families across the countryside, many from closely knit villages now physically and emotionally isolated. It's true, as Jonathan Raban suggests in *Badlands: An American Romance,* that we often sentimentalize the old European village. Levorsen's mother described life in Norway as "virtual slavery," few owning homes or "a foot of ground." Such immigrants didn't come here to be vassals again, Raban points out: "Landowners were often lonely, but there was an enviable dignity in their proprietorial solitude." And yet the solitudes described by Rolvaag, Hudson, and Hampsten evoke other feelings as well, Pauline often finding her mother crying, my own mother's memory.

The Wells County centennial history boasted of the number of farms worked by descendants of the original pioneers "who continue tilling the good earth," proud work at tremendous cost. Levorsen, too, praises the pioneers' energetic heroism but sees "lines carved by want, pain, illness and heavy labor" in the faces of adults, their children "subdued, resentful, resigned or sad." Hard times: *verachte Zeite.*

I came up on Wellsburg, a few houses, a deserted gas station and school, and passed by, probably near the Stevens Expedition's south fork crossing in 1853, thirty years before civilization arrived, forty before the frontier ended, one single wink of time. I turned north on a county gravel road, suddenly cresting a ridge to look down on the Sheyenne's valley and at a newly graded road, the older one a quarter-mile west. I coasted down, crossed the new bridge— cattle placidly moving over the old one—and drove up a half-mile to the Valley's rim where I stopped and got out.

The Sheyenne had grown since the Harvey golf-course, though still small for its ancient valley, a piece of music in a larger silence, and I wondered how we could even say we *owned* every foot of this soil. There had been what one might call a Viking, a Hamberg, a North Dakota at the bottom of a shallow sea, waters drifting in and out on a landscape adrift as well. And after ice and hot winds, dust laid down and dust picked up, drought and flood and catastrophes that still echoed like giants in the earth, we had come upon it with our hard hopes to bear the stun and struggle of those years.

Rolvaag sums up the pioneer experience: "They threw themselves blindingly into the Impossible, and accomplished the Unbelievable," and the impact of those two capitalized negatives almost says it all. The landscape had put a heavy pressure on the human life it lured and then dwarfed, promised and satisfied, promised and denied. I looked across the Valley, remembering the busy cheerfulness of Harvey and the bustle of spring planting, and then across the years in the space around and the time beneath. Below, the cattle had crossed the old bridge road and were grazing the beginnings of this year's grass. I got back in the car and moved forward, the direction of leaving waters.

I was moving one other way as well, although it was imperceptible. The massive bulk of glacial ice pressed the earth's crust down—here, one foot for every four feet of ice. That weight melting away, the crust slowly rose, an uplift still going on north in Manitoba which is sixty meters higher than it used to be. The rate of rebound is about a foot a century—six inches, then, during the lives of Mr. and Mrs. Coff, during my own life too. Thousands of travelers had moved over Wells County, itself still moving over the fluid face of the earth and slowly lifting up again, and the ice-pressed soil beneath our feet—after tears and toil and prayers—was hallowed by as much as we could possibly accomplish. Or endure.

faith in north dakota

"Faith," someone once said in the Bible, "is the substance of things hoped for, the evidence of things not seen."

"Nothing," someone once painted on a wall, "was ever lost from enduring faith in North Dakota."

I learned the first as a child and didn't know I'd come upon the other by the end of this day, that I'd travel through the faith of my fathers and perhaps the state of my own faith. I picked up the river north of Wellsburg and followed it into the bottom of Benson County, threading through the townships of East Fork, Arne, South Viking, and West Antelope. When I saw a white steeple jutting up ahead, I realized I was in the true countryside. Water towers signaled a town and grain elevators at least a railroad, but here, on gravel county roads past an occasional house, the true landmarks were churches.

I turned in the driveway and stepped out to read the bronze plaque, the Klara Evangelical Lutheran Church established in 1897, probably named for the Klaralven River in western Sweden although some folks said Nelson Olson named it for his mother. Beside it, a small cemetery lay in the morning sun and I walked through—Hakanson, Backen, Anderson, Lansrud, Strom, Pederson, Berglund—to the end of the plot walled on three sides by substantial spruce, sparrows twittering and fluttering among the branches. Beyond, in the dark, seeded fields, blackbirds raucously rose and settled again. I got back in the car, thinking of the substance of things hoped for, the evidence of things not seen.

The Baptists made sure I memorized that definition from Hebrews, so rhythmical with its balance of "things" and "things" and so dense with its Latinate hisses of "substance" and "evidence" that as a child I took the sentence itself on faith. But of what could the settlers along the Sheyenne be persuaded? What, for that matter, were my fathers, my grandfathers, certain of? How much was substance and how much was hope? *Faith of Our Fathers, Holy Faith*, our congregation sang, always a little too slowly, almost a dirge.

The closing promise droned so ploddingly that it almost hurt to sing it: *We will be true. To Thee. Til Death.*

Along with grain, the New World churches were being planted in the open space and air where every hope could find a place. Dakota writer Kathleen Norris, her spirituality formed by the Plains, quotes St. Hilary—"Everything that seems empty is full of the angels of God." Thus, for Norris, "the magnificent sky above the plains sometimes seems to sing this truth; angels seem possible in the wind-filled expanse." She finds similarities between farmers and ranchers and monks, all living in "next-year country," where a monk hauling a tank of water to an orchard—I thought of Martin Bohnet and his trees in Germantown Township—"becomes a form of prayer."

Rev. Neander, a Swedish Lutheran arriving in 1903 and later serving both the Klara and Sheyenne congregations, wrote that he'd discovered "much vacant land of good quality" and that he found "the whole state of North Dakota a large mission field," the landscape vacant first of men and then of God. But if there came different men into the empty land, there also came different Gods.

My own experience of religious conflict seems minimal now although Bill resented my mother's turn toward evangelical conservatism, taking her husband and son with her. Most of her letters to him—and to me, later—concluded with a message of salvation. "Where did we go wrong?" she once asked her sister of their two sons, first generation agnostics. But faith could do wrong as well. I remember her worry over her church's legal suit in the mid-1940s, one group of Baptists suing another for control of the church building, the court having to decide who was closer to the "true faith." My mother's group won, but she was mortified that such a division had ever taken place.

Such conflicts were often magnified on the early prairie. William Sherman reminds us in *Prairie Mosaic* that the church was a major institution in North Dakota but it also "helped to cast a shadow across the relationships" of its people, often polarizing community groups, separating families from neighbors, and causing "personal heartbreak for young people who dared to climb the walls of religious and ethnic prejudice." He's speaking of the western Dakota conflict between Orthodox Ukrainians, Presbyterians, and Catholics, but the history of Lutheranism in the countryside I drove through had as much conflict.

Because immigrants gathered together on the basis of nationality, it was difficult not to think there was something German or Norwegian or Swedish about Lutheranism, church issues attached to nationalist ones from the older world and to political ones in the newer one. It was one thing for me to walk through the peacefulness of the Klara Evangelical cemetery but another to live in those earlier years in America, Protestants and Catholics almost warring, Synods established only to divide, Presbyterians and Congregationalists breaking their union, the Presbyterians dividing into new and old schools, Mormonism, Spiritualism, and Adventism rising, waters not coming together but branching off from various divides.

Rolvaag knew such painful divisions, the struggles Lutheranism had within itself and against Irish Catholicism. *Giants in the Earth*—set in South Dakota but surely all of it Old Dakota—begins in 1873, only a couple of decades before the founding of the Klara Church, and ends with the death of Per Hansa, a secular giant in the wilderness sent by his wife through a blizzard to get a minister for a dying man, the pioneer hero dying for God, yes, but—worse perhaps—his wife's God.

The second volume concerns Per Hansa's son, *Peder Victorious*, a name given with such hubris that it makes his mother shudder. Early on, a young Peder wonders about God who perhaps was still in Norway, the Americans not needing Him, or perhaps this new land was not part of the Biblical world and God had nothing to do with it. Or God was an American, he concludes, thus Peder wanted to learn his catechism in English, horrifying his mother—imagine, "a Norwegian boy wanting to talk to God in a language his own mother can't understand."

Rolvaag titled the third volume, *Their Fathers' God,* admitting he'd considered the plural *Gods* but thinking that might be "too ironical." It would have been closer to the truth, however, as the Norwegians reflected the wide variety of viewpoints in their home country: rationalism, Puritanism, anti-clericalism, state-church loyalty, and ordinary secular indifference. The conflict between pietism and confessionalism, between good works in a good life and allegiance to the literal creed, would, for a while, divide more than it would unite.

Behind me in Wells County, Barbara Levorsen had remembered that "great rift within the Lutheran Church that set brother against brother, son against father, and neighbor against neighbor," the clashing factions of Synod and the United Branch. Similarly, the small community of Rolvaag's Spring Creek boiled with religious upheaval, the conjunction of the divisive new evangelism and an unmarried girl leaving her newborn to die. When the minister attempted to put her under church discipline and force a public confession, she committed suicide, the question of what was right according to the will of God growing "so serious that people quarreled about it until they became hoarse of voice and dark of mien, and the hand unconsciously sought a weapon."

Conflicts also burned between the Norwegian Lutherans and the Irish Catholics, Peder taking an Irish wife with disastrous results. Strong with his father's secularism, he forbids the christening of his child, although his Lutheran mother has it secretly named Peder Emmanuel and his wife, Patrick St. Olaf. Later, humiliated in politics by a Catholic opponent, Peder destroys his wife's crucifix and rosary in a rage. When he awakes, she has gone, taking their son. "I've been to the End of the World," she writes, "and have found out what it looks like. I'll never go near there again because it is an accursed place."

I took a few Benson County roads—one mile off, one mile ahead, one mile back on—to get the flavor of the land, America or Canaan or Eden, remembering the Genesis quote of Rolvaag's title: "There were giants in the earth in those days; and also after that, when the sons of God came in unto the daughters of men, and they bore children to them, the same became mighty men which were of old, men of renown."

I must have asked the Baptists years before who these giants were, and I'm sure they had an answer, perhaps a distinction between the sons of Seth and the daughters of Cain, but I no longer remembered it. One theory was that the giants were the offspring of fallen angels mating with humans, a scenario no doubt too lurid for the Baptists. Years later, I asked a professor of religion who shrugged that it was a piece of a Titan myth broken off from another faith and dropped into the Genesis narrative by one of its several authors. There was no single story.

Still, the territory I drove was large enough to contain giants. In the Bible, they're the Nephilim, a word with multiple meanings, large—Goliath could have been a descendant—or fierce, as David's most noted warriors were sometimes called, or, perhaps strangely, any debased character, any illegitimate child, or even the ghosts of the dead, the Israelites giving the name to the first inhabitants of their land who had long since disappeared. I wondered if they'd found some enormous bones and woven the story the way ancient Greeks did, finding the skulls of a few dwarf mammoths from the ice age, mistaking the trunk-opening in the skull for an eye socket, and declaring this proof of the Cyclops. But perhaps, in faith, bones are proof of nothing. A new elementary teacher told me a few years ago she couldn't use her carefully prepared unit on dinosaurs in a small North Dakota town because the Brethren-oriented community forbade it—there had been no such creatures, God putting the bones on earth only to test the people's faith.

But whether the Nephilim were giants, warriors or misshapen ancients, all I could do was take every meaning at once in the contending darkness and light of the Old Testament and of Old Dakota, driving, therefore, through the earth of the men of renown and the men unknown, the more than heroic and the only human.

Matthew said Jesus told them faith as small as a mustard seed could move mountains, an impressive but impractical miracle. Dealing with prairies and wheat would take a larger-sized faith, each year with the potential for prosperity or total defeat or, perhaps worse, with its flickers of hope, mere survival. My grandfather Charlie's faith, it seems, could have been that of a giant.

Why he left Westhope is not recorded. It was not a lack of general optimism in a town of two banks, five general stores, three hardware stores, four livery and feed stores, three hotels, and three boarding cars, along with George Johnson's lunch counter, Charlie's brother recently arrived. The First Dakota Boom had ended in 1890 and the second started around 1898, when the Klara Church had been planted, the Johnsons in their Westhope "grand mansion," at least as my mother remembered it. Charlie was a leader on the school board and, according to *The Standard,* the Johnson and Norwood store was a "hustling firm composed of young men of long experience in the front ranks of Westhope business circles."

Regarding Charlie's faith in moving one step too far west, Bill in his family history only speculated. Owning land probably offered some attractions and Charlie was tired of being a part-time banker, expected to loan money to customers and apply it to their annual bill at no interest. And there was also the mystery of Ethel, who loved horses and riding and the West—a local seamstress now "living in" with the Johnsons, a perhaps scandalous but unknowable influence, my mother and her sister tight-lipped on the subject throughout their lives, and now forever.

Whatever pushed Charlie, those were the flood years of American Progress. During the first years of my mother's life, U.S. farm prices went up more than 50 percent and the population of western North Dakota quadrupled. But for many North Dakota towns it was a "Too-Much Mistake," the abbreviated thesis of historian Robinson, too many essentials of civilization—newspapers, banks, stores—established without the population necessary to support them. When the Second Boom promised even more, it was difficult to resist the golden age of agriculture, land prices soaring in Dakota by 300 percent. People didn't know it wasn't as dry as it was going to be—they just knew it wasn't as dry as it had been. *We're marching to Zion,* some may have sung with the blessings of the government in 1909, 1912, 1916—The Enlarged Homestead Act, The Three-Year Homestead Act, The Stock-Raising Homestead Act, the last land rush, a current that moved through and pulled the Johnsons along with it, that left too much in North Dakota towns and too little on Charlie's homestead.

Ahead of me, the road disappeared, and I dipped over the edge of the Sheyenne's valley, a treeless trench with fuzzy brush in its ravines, pitched down half a mile, crossed the river, and reared a half mile back up. On top, a tractor toiled in a long field and I was again caught by the simple immensity of open space, with or without angels. I was driving through "country"—the Latin *terra contrata,* the land lying opposite, *land contrary*—and whatever happened on such journeys would be, from the same root, an *encounter*.

In our case, each encounter was farther westward, American Progress typified in the 1872 painting I'd come across from *Crofutt's New Overland Tourist and Pacific Coast Guide*. Out of the upper corner's sunrise, trains steam forward, a stagecoach in the middle, a covered wagon below, while homesteaders, miners, and farmers heartily work in the lower right foreground and buffalo and Indians move off to the left. Above this condensed earth, a woman with streaming hair and robe, a single star on her forehead, treads the air, no Christian angel but the goddess Progress. Her left hand unwinds telegraph wire, her right holds a book—the Bible or, for all the hopes given here, a railway schedule—and she glides smoothly west, countering the darkness of the countryside *that they may have Life and have it more abundantly.*

Farther northeast of the river, near Devils Lake, another kind of faith had its test as Jewish settlers arrived toward the end of the century, most of them suffering several years of harsh winters and poor crops and leaving behind only the beginnings of a Jewish cemetery. The story of Rachel Calof, one of those settlers, had been recently found, J. Sanford Rikoon helping to pass it on.

Surviving a childhood of poverty and rough work, Rachel arrived from Russia in 1894 to marry and accompany Abraham to the free land of Dakota and to his relatives. Nothing could have prepared her. She writes of the miserable shack, her dirty in-laws with wild, unshaven faces, rags wrapped around the men's feet, and the welcoming supper of boiled dough and cheese—"forty-three years later, I well remember." Brought to what Abraham had called their house, she found "four board walls, sitting in the middle of the trackless prairie." She stood and stared, unable to speak.

They lived that winter with Abraham's family, the couple's private place a pit scooped out in the center of the dirt floor, the greatest hardship of pioneer life being "the terrible crowding of many people into a small space." Close to "the living level of an animal," she survived a storm of anguish in the next few days and set to work, her first innovation molding mud into a lamp, the wick a butter-smeared rag, one little light where there had been darkness, but only one little light against that much darkness.

When Rachel had her first child, her mother-in-law's "dark beliefs"—that devils would take the baby unless she carried a knife in her belt and left a prayer-book in the cradle—soon combined with sickness and depression until Rachel herself heard demons knocking and howling at night, her husband, absent for a week at a time, not enough comfort. "Our background," Rachel writes, "was the harsh, unyielding culture of the poor and oppressed. In that world the rule of the parent was paramount, and a son did not oppose his parents' wishes." The Calofs survived the next year and the next, building up a prosperous farm in a decade until 1917, a year of "sober reflection and decision," when they decided Rachel's health and Abraham's rheumatism couldn't endure the rigors of such work. They left for the city life of St. Paul.

Rikoon reprints a photograph, a cabin to the right, Abraham atop a wagon to the left and, in the center, a small aproned figure, her face indiscernible, "Mom" handwritten above her in the blank sky that occupies two-thirds of the photo, another pioneer glimpse, poignant and terrible at once. Her son Jacob remembers more from a later scene from St. Paul: "The most vivid memory I treasure of her was the lovely picture she presented wearing her immaculate white apron over her best dress in her warm, spotless house, making her blessing over the Sabbath candles each Friday evening."

With no one to talk to along the road, I relied on last winter's reading which had included the pioneer reflections of Emil Gunsch born in 1924, his German Russian grandfather having arrived in North Dakota around 1903, the year Charlie and Esther took their picnic train-trip into the state. Emil's first pages relate his parents' success, storybook accounts of cattle and ducks, milk, eggs and potatoes, a new home built of lumber in 1918, a granary, a barn. But in 1932, the rain simply stopped, the drifting sand so high along the fences a team of horses could cross over. In 1936, no hay for the cattle, they bought thistles at ten dollars a stack and poured molasses over them. In 1937, the year I was born, the wheat on the Gunsch farm turned out to be full of rust, usable only as straw.

A decade earlier, Charlie Johnson had lost the Highline homestead, moving with Ethel to Valier, first onto a rented farm and later farther into the country, contrary-wise, where they had as little success as before. He worked in a Great Falls store, making enough money to move near Havre, trying again on a rented farm and failing again, finally getting a job with the Works Progress Administration during the Depression. "Imagine," my mother once said, "having that as the last job of your life."

But it was otherwise with Emil Gunsch, bumper crops starting in the forties as the rains returned and World War II closed off the wheat fields of Europe and Russia, and he continued with modest success and more than substantial faith. Even going blind, he wrote of his resolve to keep on working. "I believe God did this for a reason, and I'm not going to argue with Him." His reflections end with a prayer: "Now, Lord, I know that everything is well because Thou art our Master—the Truth, the Way and the Life. Amen."

Rolvaag had planned a fourth novel to present Peder Victorious coming to terms with his heritage and the new land, how "a good Catholic and a rationalistic Lutheran make out together"— remarking that he wouldn't have a friend among either the Protestants or the Catholics—but he died in 1931, the novel unwritten. Ethel Johnson died in 1940, three years after I was born, and Charlie in 1955, the year I graduated from high school. Their last prayers, if they were breathed, were not recorded, nor has any family member dared to suggest the quantity of faith remaining to them.

In Hebrews, Paul points to the greatness of men like Noah and Abraham, living by faith since they could see God's promises only from a great distance, admitting they were "strangers and pilgrims on the earth." The intensity of the Norwegian community's religion came precisely, Rolvaag writes, from "the feeling of strangeness in this alien land and the utter impossibility of striking new roots here."

This world is not my home, I used to sing with the Baptist youth on Sunday nights, which allowed more energetic tunes than the morning service. *I'm just a passer through.* But what did I know then of only passing through, of not being at home there in Colorado with friends and family, prosperous farms surrounding our small town, lifting up our eyes to the Rocky Mountains from whence, it was promised, would come our help? I had not seen my mother's prairie or Charlie Johnson's or Rachel Calof's, or that of the Norwegian giants. It's one thing to believe this world is not your home, but it's another thing to feel, as they sometimes did, that the land is not your home, that even your home is not your home.

Ahead of me at a county road intersection was a broad, freshly mown lawn and a sign for the Fron Norwegian Lutheran Church, now gone, the cemetery a thin strip along the back edge. I walked through the names—Haugen, Wold, Lindal, Tangen, Bergoust, Nels and Jenni Oksendal—and got back in my car.

Emil Gunsch's story of progress and faith was repeated by others when, during the Depression, the WPA hired people to interview Benson County pioneers, gathering more evidence of things not now seen. Margaret Medus, for example, came from Norway to help her family farm in the first drought years, married Knut Myhre, moved into his sod house, had five children and, when his health failed, drove the oxen, shocked grain, and stacked hay herself. A year after he died, she married Even Medus and together they built a church in Spring Township that, a local historian promised, "will be a memorial for years to come to the pioneer settlers of that community."

Bill Nash was also interviewed, a second-generation German remembering bad times in general: the August freezes, no rain for two summers. By 1890, "everyone was getting pretty hard up," many homesteaders leaving, the next year "make or break," and here came a bumper crop, an answer from Heaven. North

Dakota had only four good years in the next decade, but it was enough for some. "From then on," the WPA record professes, "the faith of the pioneer settlers of this section of the country was firmly established."

Now I came suddenly upon a steeple minus its church, the white sharp peak on a granite platform on a broad, grassy lawn, "Fairview Congregation" chiseled into the base. Along the fence by the field were the graves of the Guskjolens, Father and Mother born in 1878 and 1889, Husband and Wife Elmer and Gladys in 1909 and 1910. Son Bert, a sign announced, rested in Minneapolis, Daughter Luella in Everett, Washington, a third generation moving on.

A few miles later I came to the Viking Church, this one still practicing its faith, the pastors Brad and Lori Keyser-Boswell, their first names and the hyphenated last an assurance we were all in the last of the twentieth century. I walked through the cemetery—many births between the 1860s and '80s, deaths in the 1920s and '30s—and stopped by the stone for the Branvolds: Christ (1868–1930) and Tilda (1869–1929), born a year apart and dying a year apart, who'd spoken in Norwegian verse to the child they'd sent ahead years before:

> *Sov sadt du kjeve i stille grav*
> *et bedre livdid herren gav*
> *du hivile som barnet i modern's favn*
> *og vagne du skat i himmelin's havn.*

I repeated the verse out loud, not knowing the language but with an idea of "stille grav" and "himmelin's havn." Later, I found someone to translate: "Sleep softly, dear child, in your quiet grave; the Lord has given you a better life. You will rest like a child in its mother's embrace and enter safely into the harbor of heaven."

Suffer the little ones to come unto Me. And suffer them to leave as well.

It was quiet across the countryside except for a tractor here and there, and I passed cemeteries at about the same frequency, driving through present work and past memorials, a word from the Latin for "mindful" so that *to remember* was to fill one's mind with what had passed away, one's mother, one's grandmother, the country before this one, the ancient Nephilim. Remember us, they didn't have the power to say anymore, but we did, or we tried, because we knew we set out each day only from the past. The old Norse giant who guards the well of wisdom is named Mimir, the echo of being full of memory.

A little before noon, I headed into the northwest tip of Eddy County and arrived at the town of Sheyenne—three hundred citizens now, five hundred in the 1950s—which reflected a past makeover, the buildings along the main street westernized with brown, rustic false-fronts. "Take the Historic Walking Tour," a weathered billboard read so when I dropped by the Tastee Freeze on Main Street to get a hamburger I asked the cook about it. Oh, she shrugged, that was when they had that Bicentennial. There used to be a brochure but they were out. She guessed I could walk around and read whatever signs were still on the buildings—they'd say what each one used to be. Like the Tastee Freeze here? Used to be the old Fire Hall.

After eating, I walked down the boardwalk, my shoes clattering a little hollowly in the quiet, stopping to read about the restaurant that became a shoe repair shop that turned into a drug store. Now it was Old Country Gifts and Floral, but not quite now, because it was closed up and for sale. Down the block, I found the Sheyenne Bar open, and stepped inside. One customer sat at the bar with a draught of beer and the bartender introduced himself as Marv, a Norwegian Lutheran, "full-blooded," he said. They were always glad to have visitors. So what was I doing around here? Well, I'd been looking for historic places, stopping at cemeteries, that kind of thing, just looking at the land.

"You a geologist or something?" Marv asked. "Or you just like to look for old stuff?"

I hesitated, wondering what exactly I was, what I was looking for. The moment hung in the air. "Old stuff," I said.

Well, then I should hear this story. Marv leaned on the bar. He used to work in aerial spraying and one time he landed in a field and this guy nearby said, "Come on over here, show you something," so he went over and there was this huge rock half split open with some kind of big fierce sonuvabitch fossil inside. So Marv said what the guy should do is get some scientist out to tell him what it was. Well, twenty years later, Marv met that guy again running the bar over at Hamar and asked if he'd ever found out about that rock and, do you know, he never did anything? Just left it in the field and plowed around it each year. Marv shook his head and stepped back. Then he leaned forward again.

Now about twenty years ago the county was building a road over a hill just west of town and they hit, must have been, an Indian burial ground. The bodies were sitting up, packed around with black dirt. Now that hill is all clay, you know, so they must have brought it up from the river, some kind of special belief to do all that work. The workmen were just laying the bones beside the road and the woman that owned the land tried to get somebody to figure out what to do. They asked the Sioux and the Sioux said it wasn't theirs and the workmen just kept laying the bones out and, well, that couldn't go on, so the woman gathered them all up, dug a hole, and buried them.

You know, my fellow patron remembered, this was a long time ago by now, but they were tearing down a church here. They didn't have any use for the windows, and they were these nice, pretty church windows? So he took them home and stored them in a chicken coop. But, golly, he hadn't thought of them in a long time. He paused. Well, they were probably not in too good a shape by now, he decided, shaking his head, sounding a little sorry he'd forgotten them. Then—speaking of graves. He once found three outside of a church cemetery, suicides. "That's how you can tell—they didn't let 'em be buried in the church ground."

"Yeah, they did that to bastard kids, too," Marv put in. "Oh, yeah, some girl gets knocked up and the kid dies, they do that."

"Well," the customer took a sip of beer and shook his head, "they came over from the Old Country and to them the church was the most important thing. That's why they did some of those things."

We all looked down at the bar. I had scattered thoughts of the beliefs we hold, the ones we lose, the ones left behind almost accidentally. Our fathers had put their faith in—God? Progress? Wheat? Each other? This world might not be our home, but we had to live here whether or not we were marching on to Zion and however we moved among the many evidences of things no longer seen.

You know, Marv remembered suddenly, there used to be a baby's grave on a hill on his property, a piece of wood said 1889. He used to plow carefully around it but, he shrugged, you know. He sold the land and these days they use such big farm equipment they just dragged it over. You couldn't tell where it was now, that was for sure. Oh, yeah, the customer said. No use trying to find it now. All three of us looked down at the bar again, a moment of silence for all things lost.

I drove out on the main street, slowing past a cabin, "1867," in a little park, and slowing even more to read a slogan, sponsored by a bank and painted on a brick building in large letters only slightly faded: "Nothing was ever lost through enduring faith in North Dakota." Well, yes and no, I guessed, picking up speed and leaving a variety of faiths behind, humming a few hymns on my way home, finding I'd forgotten a lot of the words.

spirit lake, spirit heart

A few weeks after talking to Marv, I picked up the river a few miles east of Sheyenne winding through grassy pasture, a few Herefords drowsing under a few cottonwoods on the other bank, the southern boundary of the Devils Lake Sioux reservation. I stopped by a bridge and climbed through brush to kneel down. Blasts of straw and sticks in the bushes recorded the high level of a spring flood—I'd have been thrashing in six feet of icy water—and pointed the way it went. I dabbled my hand in the water, hello, and climbed back up to the road, not knowing I'd be thinking about floods most of the day.

I drove a few miles, a black highway becoming a blue one, then turned north onto a gravel road into the reservation. I was letting the Sheyenne continue while I wandered a little, looking for two hearts I'd found on the map—Devils Heart Butte, a matter of science, and, toward the far end, old Iron Heart, a post office and hotel at an intersection of trails or, most likely now, a patch of grass in empty sunlight. And maybe the butte wasn't even a butte. State geologist John Bluemle thought it might be better described as a sand volcano.

In local glacial history, the last one down gouged out the basin of the lake, the left-over debris now rolling hills, and weighed so heavily upon the land that when it lightened, groundwater under pressure found a weak spot, erupting watery sand and gravel into the smooth cone of a hill. Bluemle had seen it happen on a crew drilling into a shallow aquifer that blew out salty water they barely contained to ruin only one field's crops. It happened in the 1880s as well: a drilling crew dropping a railroad rail down as a plug, watching as it suddenly shot back up. Such force would explain the almost perfect arch of the hill I now saw one-quarter section ahead and one over, the *mini wakan chante,* "the heart of the enchanted water," according to Nicollet, the French geographer who passed by in 1839.

I didn't think I'd climb it, probably on fenced land, but when I arrived a gate was open, a two-track path leading across the field, and no warning signs. I edged up, saw nothing I might be violating and drove into the field, grasses grazing the Escort's undercarriage. The road went on but I stopped at the base of the hill, slipped my jacket on against the slight breeze, grabbed my camera bag, and started up. The grade was fairly steep so I stopped to catch my breath and take a picture of my tiny distant car, the new automatic-advance mechanism snapping loudly.

Sitting down on the gravelly slope, I looked east across the reservation, a space with history before we knew there were histories, grasslands, veldts, forests, and lakes in succession. Hunters of mammoths and giant bison moved through, followed eight or nine thousand years ago by those practicing a modern life we now call Archaic and leaving scattered points and blades. The next wave of immigrants called Woodland, their leavings broken pottery. A thousand years ago, square earth-lodges appeared along the Missouri, then years of rounding into circles, and then we came, calling ourselves Historic.

On our first contact maps the Sioux—Lakota, Dakota, Yankton, and Yanktonai—were written in between the Red and the Missouri, the Sheyenne River a small boundary between them and the Chippewa who tended to stay north and northeast in the Red River Valley. The reservation's five towns explain the rest of the history—the military Fort Totten, the Roman Catholic mission of St. Michael, and the three 1906 Great Northern Railroad sites of Hamar, Warwick, and Tokio—soldiers, Christians, and railroaders converging on this oasis of the plains, its lakes and ponds rich with fish and beaver, its timbered slopes and small valleys a thousand homes to elk, bear, and wolf. The breeze sharpened a little and I zipped my jacket as I stood up. One more push would make it.

When I came up on the summit I took a sudden step backward. In the valley below stood a log-fenced circle, a large pole in the center fluttering with the ribbons and feathers of a Sioux flag. The tire-tracks I'd seen came curving around the base of the hill and straight to the circle, another set converging from the west, a hidden place of gathering. Feeling exposed, I flattened down, almost hitting a tobacco can half-buried in the glacial gravel, an offering to some holiness below and around me.

For a few moments, looking down at the grassy mystery, I was a privileged viewer. I lifted my camera, aimed it, and pushed the button. The automatic-advance mechanism snapped like a rifle's ricochet and I was instantly self-conscious. Sprawled, peering over the rim, I could have been an enemy scout or a white soldier. Embarrassed, I slid my camera into its bag. A week or so later, I told a Mandan acquaintance what I'd seen. Probably a burial ground, she frowned. Did I take any pictures? Oh, no, I lied. Later, I found the one photo and scissored it to bits.

Finally nothing but an intruder, I turned and zigzagged down. I'd gone up for the sake of earth's science and come back for the sake of people's history, something sacred around. I let myself back into the car, closed the door gently, and drove out, someone else's grass whisking against the car, bending forward and, after I passed, straightening up again.

For years, my limited world was empty of the First People. Once, in nineteenth-century Nebraska, my father's mother looked out the kitchen window at an Indian looking in, causing her to scream and run out of the house, no one to be seen. And once my mother with her sister and brother-in-law were stalled in the old Dodge coming back from the Valier farm in Montana, when two Indians came out of the woods, circled the car, scowled, and went back into the woods. That was all, these two ghostly manifestations the only reminder of what I thought was the past.

I wasn't taught about Indians in school and knew about "what happened" only in vague generalities. Late junior high, I happened on John Collier's *Indians of the Americas,* stunned by its first sentences: "They had what the world has lost. They have it now. What the world has lost, the world must have again, lest it die." I read on, horrified, "no method of destruction not used," especially on the Plains Indians against whom "a policy of annihilating of the societies and then of the individual Indian personality was carried to the farthest extreme." When I put down that book in 1950, I was living in a different world. Have you heard about this? I asked friends, teachers, parents. Well, yes, it was too bad, it really was. But that was in the past, they pointed out, and for a while, I'm sorry to say, I believed them.

I was twenty-six before the past came into my view as well as the present, in a high school gym in Fairbanks, Alaska, for the beginning of the "Eskimo Olympics." The first real drums I'd heard began to throb and a line of dancers stepped from a side door onto the varnished floor. The first, fierce, high note of song sent a thrill up my spine, a combination howl and hymn, protest and acceptance, defiant survivors following the U.S. flag around a gym as if they moved at the center of the world, for me the Grand Entry of an entire nation.

Coming to North Dakota with its four reservations, I discovered I was a *wasichu,* a white, although I could never quite get a fix on its literal meaning. "Fat-stealers," a Chippewa woman once told me, after the soldiers' habit of stealing the best meat from the drying racks, but others said they didn't know, perhaps a kind lie about something worse. *Wasichu* or not, I'd read last winter about Devils Lake and its people. I mean, its People.

Only the Cuthead Yanktonai lived nearby in 1867 when another link of military occupation was forged—Fort Totten joining the chain of Fort Abercrombie on the Red, Buford and Stevenson on the Missouri, and Ransom on the southern bend of the Sheyenne. Two traders and an interpreter fanned out to invite Sioux "peacefuls," as they were called. But earlier, the area had attracted "hostiles," as they were more frequently called, Sisseton and Wahpeton Dakota fleeing as refugees after the 1862 Minnesota

Massacre or Sioux Uprising, the headwaters of the wars on the northern plains that, rising and turning, would carry Indian and *wasichu* alike to a circle of fire in the snow at Wounded Knee.

Reading of the uprising was like standing on a shore, watching a current in and out of control. The Chippewa, pressured themselves, gradually push some Wahpeton and Sisseton into the woods and prairies of the Minnesota valley where, forced to cede land to the *wasichu*, about seven thousand gather along the Minnesota River on the Upper and Lower agencies. By 1857, the currents increase, settlers tight around the boundaries and urging a further reduction of Indian lands. And another two years for Congress to decide on payment of which, after the claims of traders, the Upper Sioux receive half, the Lower Sioux almost nothing.

The waters surge around a cut bank in 1860, Civil War rising in the east, soldiers leaving for the battlefields, a temptation in Minnesota. The crops fail in 1861 and the winter is hungry, cold even around the fires. In 1862, the government's promised provisions are weeks late, then a month, then two months. When the Indians protest, storekeeper Andrew Myrick says, overheard and repeated: "If they're hungry, let them eat grass."

The tributaries begin to merge near a homestead a few miles from Grove City when four young men—already outsiders, Upper Sioux married to Lower—return from a hunt, falling into some small whirlpool of argument that begins with taunts about bravery and ends with the death of five settlers. The news spreads, groups assemble at Little Crow's village for advice and, although he's often sided with the *wasichu*, he finally agrees to war, whatever he thinks of their chances. The morning of August 18, the Lower Agency is attacked, thirteen killed including Andrew Myrick, his body found later, his mouth stuffed with grass.

Such a flood always runs unpredictably, taking one kind of turn here, another there, rolling around a corner to smash against a rocky cliff, rebounding to leave a sapling untouched. Some are killed, some go free. The Sioux loot some cabins or take some cattle and horses and, when they leave, freebooting whites complete the pillage of their fellow citizens. The river runs on—a battle at New Ulm, Birch Coulee, Wood Lake—and then thins and dissipates, Sioux uprising, uprisen, and gone.

The trials of prisoners are quick, evidence flimsy, 307 sentenced to death. President Lincoln makes a distinction between murderers and those merely present by approving death sentences for only thirty-nine—still the largest mass execution in U.S. history—which only disappoints most Minnesotans and embitters the Sioux, who considered themselves prisoners of war. Some flee toward Devils Lake, bringing General Sibley into Dakota the next year to cross the Sheyenne and ultimately expand the Indian Wars of the 1860s onto the plains. Standing on a shoreline, that is what it looks like when history acts like water.

By that time, General Pope observes, the Indian country is penetrated everywhere, highways cut through, the game gone. "The Indians are therefore crowded more and more into narrow limits," he reports, "where they are less able every day to subsist themselves by hunting. Of course, they are becoming exasperated and desperate and avail themselves of every opportunity to rid their country of the whites." *Of course*, the General writes.

It was, therefore, mainly starvation and desperation in 1867 that brought about fifty-seven lodges—something like two hundred fifty men, women, and children—to Ft. Totten, growing to over four hundred in the next couple of years. Early settlement was band-oriented, the Yanktonai in the Crow Hill area and the Sisseton and Wahpeton in the vicinities of St. Michael, Tokio, and Woodlake. Intermarriage blurred such distinctions but settlement continued that way into the 1920s and, for that matter, I still heard echoes. In the gas station at St. Michael, a woman said, "Oh, those people at Crow Hill," pursing her lips in that direction with an opinion I didn't understand. And a Ft. Totten man once grinned, "Yeah, those people living in Tokio," shaking his head and winking, meaning something else I didn't understand.

The next decade was a push of what we called Progress although an unnamed countercurrent swirled near in 1868 when a dozen or so warriors surrounded the garrison mules grazing west of the fort buildings and retreated from the rifle fire of soldiers, none of whom knew the leader as an up and coming warrior, *Tatanka Iyotake* to the Sioux or, as the *wasichu* would later never forget, Sitting Bull.

But this was only one incident—the mainstreams here held the blended currents of Christianity and Agriculture, each with its ironies and conflicts. The 1867 Treaty allowed compensation only for "services," few possible except forced farming. The 1869 appropriation was a tin cup of corn, a bucket of seed potatoes, and one seed packet each of carrot, beet, turnip, and rutabaga but it arrived too late to plant and the winter brought near starvation. By the time William Forbes, the first Ft. Totten agent, arrived the next year, twenty adults had died of malnutrition.

Nor was God's progress simple. When the Office of Indian Affairs parceled out The People to the various tribes of Christianity, the Catholics got the Dakota, or vice versa, so that in 1874 four Grey Nuns arrived from the Sisters of Charity in Montreal to set up a boarding school. Thus, Dakota children, perhaps staring but more likely looking down, sat listening to Catholic nuns teach in French through English interpreters.

That same year the Secretary of the Interior, apparently in charge of theories of civilization, identified as barbarous whatever destroyed what he called individuality. "Where everything is held in common, thrift and enterprise have no stimulus or reward and thus individual progress is rendered very improbable if not impossible."

By now the Sioux were somewhat self-sufficient through communal gardening but that wasn't enough. A life held in common was set up in America's gun-sights, what Collier meant when he spoke of the annihilation of the Indian personality. The 1887 Allotment Act cut reservations into shape—160 acres to each family head or single individual over 21—and sold-off anything left, a solution that quickly became a larger problem that still exists. No method available to settle individual claims except sell the allotment and divide the money among the heirs, only about a quarter of the land here is held by the tribe. According to Collier, Indians nationwide lost 90 million acres through land allotment from 1887 to 1933—"but in addition, they lost to whites the *use* of most of the allotted land still owned."

Not only did the *wasichu* know how land should be owned, they knew what to put in it—wheat, that golden grain of Progress that needed 12 to 17 inches of rain and, for a while, received it. This enterprise would also quite nicely erode Sioux family life, sex-roles, values, and habits. By 1879, the Fort Totten agent, satisfied with the progress of wheat-farming in dissolving traditional practices, proudly claimed that "Each family labors by themselves and for themselves. Nothing is held in common."

By 1883, it was Good Times, the peak of the First Dakota Boom. A bit farther west, grassland was opened up for grazing. The Marquis de Mores, our most famous European outsider, named the town of Medora for his wife and started a cattle empire and meat distribution center. Rough and rugged Theodore Roosevelt developed his ranch north of Medora and felt "strong as a bear" now that he could do cowboy work. But history kept winding. Payments to the Dakota ended as crop failures grew more common on land less their own. Drought burned the earth while it hatched grasshoppers and one after another intensely cold winter arrived. In 1886 a drought summer arrived, then winter six weeks early, freezing cattle, killing hopes. The Marquis de Mores retreated to France—his village deserted in three years—and Roosevelt found himself unable to enjoy his western ranch. "I shall be glad to get home," he admitted.

The army marched away from Ft. Totten in 1890 when half of the *wasichu* farms in the state were mortgaged and the drought-struck Dakota lived mainly on parched corn and turnips. The next year, forty adults died from "destitution." The next year, seventy. The Dakota, the Ft. Totten agent sympathetically wrote, had done "what even experienced white farmers with better advantages have done—signally failed in agriculture for the last number of years." But the white farmers had the final advantage of leaving, many abandoning their claims and moving to Minnesota, reversing the westward course of empire, dismayed at where the currents had taken them.

By the turn of the century, American Progress had done almost as much as it could for and against the First People and it didn't get much better in the 1930s or the following decades, because they lived on lands so divided it was often impossible to sustain farming or ranching. Federal policy advocated leasing land to non-Indians, which provided the ultimate irony—a Dakota forced to lease sometimes ended up working for a *wasichu* farmer on his own land.

It didn't all depend on agriculture, of course, and the talk these days was about income from gaming or expanding industries, like the pre-cast concrete company already in the Fort Totten industrial park, but by this time the same talk went on in the small *wasichu* towns as well, questions of economic survival on the northern plains no matter what tribe one belonged to.

So this was their history and partly mine, because my forebears had seen one or two of the People who disappeared and because I had seen their Grand Entry as well and I knew they were here. Devils Lake had always been considered more "Indian" or "pagan" than the other reservations—even in 1937, my birth year, a large fullblood element was officially noted—and there was here a certain persistence of what the world at large had lost, in Collier's words, including a program in the schools to reintroduce the Dakota language. Sometimes, after a Catholic funeral, a second ceremony was held in the round house. I could accidentally look over a ridge into a valley of tradition as I had this morning at Spirit Heart or, as I'd done a few years ago, drive a quarter-mile off the road and spend the night in another sacred world.

It had been arranged, my friend told me, an *inipi,* my first sweat lodge. She'd been invited for Sunday night and she could bring a guest. What should I wear? I asked her, suddenly nervous. What was it like? How would I know what to do? A bathing suit, she shrugged, answering only the first question.

Inviting outsiders to such ceremonies is no longer done and I understand. Worried later about describing that night, I consulted Ambrose Little Ghost, a spiritual leader on the Spirit Lake Reservation. He said I could write of my own experience, not that of others, and I agreed, that being my only intention.

That night, by the time she turned on a dirt lane and turned again, I only knew I was south of the lake. A piece of cloth on a mailbox marked the final turn up a quarter-mile, two-track path to get to the house and, behind it, the huge pit, the fire going all day, driftwood from the lake shore blazing around smooth granite boulders. Since the *inipi* would begin at sundown I thought we'd get to eat first, not the case, and I practiced being hungry while standing with strangers who knew each other.

Finally, the fire brighter as shadows of trees moved out and slowly covered us, an older man gave instructions in a Dakota voice, soft vowels and husky consonants brushing like wind in grass. First would be the offering, and he provided a half-palm of tobacco from a can of Sir Walter Raleigh. We walked around the blaze, offering tobacco in each of the four directions, and I tried to make myself feel holy, to separate my human nature from the sacred, the way I'd been taught religion demanded. Ahead of me, a Dakota woman, more at home, casually ambled in shower clogs around the circle, scattering the sacred tobacco from one hand while she puffed on a Marlboro from the other.

Following eight or nine others, I crawled into the sweat lodge, a small dome of curved willow branches, layered with hides and blankets, and sat on the hard dirt floor, just room enough. A pipe was passed around and, as we lifted it, we looked around the circle. "To all my relations," we said, meaning everyone in the lodge and maybe everyone else in the world. Then a half dozen or so stones were raked in from the fire, truly white hot, a bright milky glare radiating from the small pit.

I'd been given a clump of sage and told I should cup it in my hand and breathe through it if the air got too hot. One pour of water over the glowing stones and it got too hot—the lodge filled with a cloud of fiercely suffocating steam, searing my nostrils and lungs while I sucked gulps of air through the sage. I could leave, but I was afraid of disturbing others and I had a measure of pride—

I hadn't come to a sweat lodge only to leave when it got hot. Still, it was getting even hotter. Worried I might pass out, I concentrated on the throb of the small drum, the first high thrill of song I remembered from Alaska, and then the wavering descent of melody, fading in and out as I wavered and faded in the heat.

When the first "round" was over and the hides and blankets were tossed away from the doorway, I staggered into the cooler night air, thankful I was alive. My friend agreed she'd had no idea of the intensity of that heat, observed that it was an interesting thing to have done, and walked back to the house. I stood a few yards away, cooling off, listening to the drumbeat and singing of the second round and, when the doorway was thrown open for the third, I was ready to crawl inside that darkness again. To all my relations.

It was a world where ordinary things became sacred, and then ordinary, and then sacred again. The third round was a healing ceremony for two women. At some important moment, the singer yanked at the willow framework above his head, the tent flapping fiercely around us, making my heart leap and both of the women almost convulse. He was not pretending spirits were doing this, his hands clearly visible, but it felt like something more was happening in the thundering of our small-domed universe. It was not magic turning out to be a trick—it was a trick turning out to be magic.

The doorway was opened again, cool night air slipping inside, and someone left and someone entered and the stones for the last round were raked in, the doorway closed, the water poured, another searing cloud of purification welling up. Able now to endure the thick heat but still dazed, I found myself staring at one of the glowing white cobbles, a blue spot widening and spreading as if it were inside the rock. No doubt the color changed as the rock cooled, I thought, but I continued to stare at it, the blue spot larger and brighter, then appearing to move, not inside the rock anymore or even on its surface but wavering up and down in front of me, wings pulsing back and forth. I thought my eyes had fixated on an illusion, so I shut them for a moment and when I opened them saw only the reddish-white stones in front of me. The song ended and the doorway was thrown open again.

Afterward, my body strangely light, both warm and cool, the fragrance of sage still in my nostrils, I edged up to a group of men just to listen in.

"Hoo, did you see that bluebird in there?" one asked. "It was flying all *over* the place." Another nodded and grinned knowingly.

A shiver went through me at the word "bluebird" and I stood, staring over the sweat lodge and into the dark trees. I didn't want to be a believer or, I realized then, a non-believer. We all walked back to the house where a large potluck supper had been set out and I ate ravenously. We left about midnight and it was hard to imagine waking up the next morning at home in a valley to the east. It felt like a thousand miles away and maybe that many years.

When I came to North Dakota—the year John Collier died, although I didn't know it then—I wondered about the name Devils Lake which carried a *wasichu* scent a mile off, our way of calling nature the Devil's This and Hell's That. The year after I left, the tribe voted to rename itself "Spirit Lake Nation," the town keeping its Christian name, its high school team The Satans.

The first name was *Mni-wakan,* "Bad Water," if you believed it referred to the lake's salinity, or, more likely, "sacred or mysterious water," but these couldn't compete with an Evil Spirit. One rainy night in a Devils Lake motel I'd found the legend on the rack of free tourist information. Sioux and Chippewa, camped on opposite sides of the lake, decided to attack secretly at night, a forbidden practice. When they fell into battle, the lake turned red with blood and a huge wave drowned them all. "From that day on an Evil Spirit dwells within the lake." I stood by the lobby's Coke machine looking outside, a farmer's pickup gleaming in the rain, a Dakota boy standing under the motel canopy, hands in the pockets of his jeans jacket, while huge drops fizzed in the puddles of the parking lot. "The Evil One," the story ended, "waits patiently for an Indian to paddle a canoe on the water so that he may overturn the canoe and claim the Indian for his own."

Although the brochure's story of Good versus Evil was couched in pseudo-mythological language, what was actually happening with the lake could support a theory of evil, causing more than one Dakotan to invoke the name of God. If war could be like water, water could be like war.

As I drove slowly east toward Iron Heart, I knew what was going on above me. Last summer I'd barely made it across The Narrows, a dike-road they'd been forced to raise. Dakota men in fluorescent orange vests flagged traffic into a single lane as trucks dumped out boulders and bulldozers flattened earth, the camouflage uniforms of the National Guard announcing a renewed military presence on the grounds of the fort, the waves of the good or bad lake splashing against new dirt and rocks.

Most of the time we can't help feeling our little blink of life is the stability of the world. Not so, of course. The ice age waters were three times the size of Devils Lake before they flooded away down valleys like the ancient Sheyenne. The smaller lake left behind had its own tides, shrinking to nothing half a dozen times in the last 4,000 years and filling again, a dry bed a hundred years before Christ and so full by the 1800s that it and Stump Lake, now more than five miles away, were probably one body of water that sometimes spilled into the Sheyenne. Settlers pitchforked fish from the teeming waters into their wagons and steamboats carried people, mail, and supplies to Church's Ferry and Minnewakan, towns later a highway drive away.

Then the waters began to lower. The citizens of West End, a speculative site awaiting the railroad, had built a wharf four hundred feet long into Devils Lake for steamboat traffic, then watched the railroad pass and the lake retreat, their pier a lumbered whale out of water. In 1924 the Narrows were little more than a mud flat; Mr. Young at the North Dakota Biological Station explained this was simply "the fate of so many other glacial lakes in North America." He even chanced an analogy: "The youth and maturity of Devils Lake are past, the period of old age has arrived." By 1940, the lake had dropped about thirty-five feet, an enormous difference in shoreline. The question was how to replenish Devils Lake to salvage a failing recreation industry, and the answer was a project to ditch Missouri River water eastward. What happened instead was the devil's own fluctuation.

The lake rose at mid-century, then fell, up in the '70s, down in the early '90s, then up, more rain falling for longer periods, groundwaters rising. In 1993, farmers in the basin lost more than 20 percent of their crops, almost the same in 1994. Last summer when I'd driven across the Narrows, mud flats before I was born, the water stood at 1,431 feet, up thirteen in the last two years, the highest in more than a century.

The lake might again be part of the Hudson Bay system. Fourteen more feet and it would spill over and include Stump Lake; twenty one more and it would gush into the Sheyenne, two-thirds of the town of Devils Lake underwater. We had thought of using the Sheyenne as an outlet before but that meant into the Red and into Canada, which made clear its concerns about non-indigenous fish and diseases and who knew what else. Still, you had two choices—store more water in the basin or send it downstream.

By the end of last summer—the *wasichu* government sending more than 20 million dollars of flood relief—nobody knew what would happen. Another two feet next year would do fifty million dollars damage. Last spring, in the icy rain I'd felt beside the Sheyenne's ambiguous headwaters, the lake had risen half an inch a day, then an inch. In mid-May, a low-pressure system moved across in a steady drizzle, fields above water too wet to plant and, anyway, too cold for germination. Fields below water, well, Lawson Jones, who farmed near the homestead site of Rachel Calof, told a reporter he'd lost a thousand acres two years ago, almost that last year. "I got more debts than I ever had," he said. "It's a little scary."

This summer, crews had cut dirt roads in two to drain the fields toward Devils Lake. Thirty families on the reservation had to move. Side roads washed out and blacktop roads crumbled apart as heavy traffic detoured over them, emergency access cut off to many of the 6,000 people of the Spirit Lake Nation. June had brought more thunderstorms, water flowing in from the drainage area at two thousand cubic feet a second, the lake now about 80,000 acres, doubled in three years.

It hit town and country alike. Homes had pressed closer to a shrinking lake and now the lake pressed back, a hundred houses moved by now. Farmer John Grann lost 7,000 of his 8,000 acres—

"We have no choice but to get out of the way," he said. Sixty-six-year-old Bobby Michels announced he was selling, leaving the house he'd been born in. A reporter asked why he wouldn't leave the land to his son. "I don't hate him that bad," Michels replied.

"We are in the hands of God here," noted Senator Kent Conrad from high atop the wall between Church and State, and the U.S. Army Assistant Secretary for Civil Works agreed—"What I'm praying for here is divine intervention." Geologist Bluemle wrote an article reminding everyone that the rising and falling of the lake was its "natural condition."

A year after I left Dakota, I phoned a friend to check out the lake's progress. The Narrows road had gone under, he reported, the fifteen-mile trip between Ft. Totten and Devils Lake now about forty, hundreds of people relocated. I asked if there was a plan. Well, store more water in the basin, for one thing. And, he said, maybe an outlet to the Sheyenne.

I was looking for Iron Heart that late afternoon because Doug Wick had said there were still ruins there and I'm lured by any survival. Probably a veteran of the 1862 Uprising, Iron Heart had converted to Christianity and then to enterprise, building a mail station and hotel at the southeast end of the lake, a couple miles north of the Sheyenne. Following the section numbers and a map, I came to an empty field with an empty dirt road and turned north.

Curving through woods a few miles, down one sandy hill and up another, I came to a clearing of tall pasture grass with a dilapidated shack at the far edge, roof caved in, siding torn away, a nest of plastered lath about to be reclaimed by the oak and sumac

behind it. I waded through the grass to step inside, sunlight splin-
tering into bars of light and shade across the gritty floor, and then
outside through the collapsing rear wall. A log cabin sank almost
flat beneath the grass, its roof boards thick with lichen, and a trail
slipped over the ridge and disappeared in the dry thickets below.
This had to be that crossroads, the Ft. Totten trail west, the
Pembina to the northeast, the Ft. Abercrombie trail southeast with
its turnoff to a Hudson Bay Company in Minnesota and, eventually, to St. Paul, another complete world away.

Elsewhere waters were rising, trouble was brewing, but this
hidden place seemed calm. I walked back through the broken
house again and sat down on the front step, the late afternoon sun
across the grass. I was in the realm of dereliction, a word legally
signifying land left permanently dry by receding waters, but here
land made into a space by the advancing and receding movements
of a local history, a rough pasture with a broken mail station left
stranded, high and dry.

It was all completely natural, this rise and fall, but it was not
easy for us to live with this nature. It was hard to lose one's home
after some years. It was hard to lose one's land after some centuries. I remembered what Mary Jane Schneider, an Indian Studies
professor in North Dakota, had said about cycles. The 1934 Indian Reorganization Act emphasized cultural survival—thanks in
part to John Collier's work—but the 1953 plan called for termina-
tion of all reservations, then the 1975 act emphasized Indian sov-
ereignty and self-determination. Thus, the one apparent constant
was that federal Indian policies changed drastically every twenty
or thirty years, a tide moving in and moving out.

Imagine these cycles continuing, I thought, leaning back on a
post in the sunlight. Or imagine them ending. Last June, a white
buffalo calf had been born on Dan and Jean Shirek's farm. It died

a month later but, amazingly enough, another was born there in July. White Buffalo Calf Woman, who gave the Dakota the sacred pipe, promised that the seventh generation would make them stand strong again and that four white buffalo would appear as a sign. One had been born in Wisconsin in 1994, another two years later on the Pine Ridge Reservation, and this one in Dakota. One more remained to be born. This was the seventh generation. When White Buffalo Calf Woman left, she turned into a black buffalo calf, then a red one, then yellow, and finally white, before disappearing into the distant grasses or the air. Sitting in that Heart, in the back and forth washing of light and shadow, I had an idea what kind of grass and what kind of air that would happen in, and why one would watch for something to return.

with heraclitus and nicollet on the sheyenne

A few weeks later, the day bright and breezy, I drove west from the Red River Valley on Highway 15 with something very particular to look for, the spot circled on my map where Joseph Nicollet, a French geographer on his way into U.S. history, had crossed the Sheyenne. Heraclitus warned us— he warned someone—that we could never step into the same river twice. But I wanted to step into the same river 150 years later.

Nicollet came to the United States in 1832, a mathematician and astronomer with an interest in "the observation sciences," as they were called. America offered wonderfully unmapped territory and he spent the rest of his life working on his grand scheme, a map of the entire Mississippi system. He traveled through the South and then up to the Great Lakes, spending the winter months of 1836–1837 near Fort Snelling in Minnesota, sometimes staying in the home of a certain Henry H. Sibley who would later, as a general, follow a fragment of Nicollet's journey for other reasons.

Finally, Nicollet was allowed to lead two official government expeditions: in 1838, to the Coteau des Prairies in eastern South Dakota and, a year later—with a young John Frémont as assistant—from Fort Pierre on the Missouri in South Dakota over the prairies to the Sheyenne, turning north to Devil's Lake, and then to Minnesota. His work provided the first accurate chart of the plains between the Mississippi and the Missouri, the 1842 *Map of the Hydrographical Basin of the Upper Missouri.* Hydrography. Latin and Greek seem scientifically abstract now, but their physical origins are easily found, the root of *hydro* the ancient *wed* or *wod* of the Indo-European, which is heard and felt in "water," "wash," and "wet," the splash of liquid. And the way we graphed our letters years ago made cut or scratch the logical verb. Thus, attempting the science of hydrography, we try to carve in some definite form the indefinite washing of rivers. We try to write down water.

I'd been reading Nicollet's journal last winter when I came to a footnote, a startling certainty in a commonplace tone: "Nicollet crossed the Sheyenne in T150N, R62W, Sec. 26, Eddy County, N. Dak., where there is now an unimproved road crossing." I let the book fall back in my lap. A historic spot I had never heard of was less than a hundred miles west of my house, located by a grid's fact and a dirt road precisely there. I had the key to a secret knowledge, and today I was moving toward it, taking special notice of where I was.

An Eddy County map lay beside me so when I passed a large wetland on my left I knew its name—the Omlid Slough—and also that it was perfectly intersected by the 98th meridian. Because this was the first time I knew my exact longitude, I pulled off at the side of the road. Such crossings should not be taken lightly. On a globe, the 98th meridian comes out of Antarctica's Seraph Bay, glides over ocean until it reaches Mexico, enters Texas, joins Highway 81 through most of Oklahoma, splits Kansas, slices Nebraska's Central City and South Dakota's Mitchell, slides up the eastern side of North Dakota and over Lake Winnipeg in Canada to finally enter, beyond the Sverdrup Islands, the pure center of the Arctic. Here, this sunny morning in Nelson County, it divided the Omlid Slough's sparkling, sky-filled water and waving green rushes. Mallards and wood ducks bobbed on the choppy water while red-winged and yellow-winged blackbirds clung to bending reeds or scattered up briefly, then settled again.

I couldn't imagine a line precisely crossing this wetland sprawl where water and reeds gave way to small bays and inlets surrounding islands of grass and soaked marsh earth containing smaller and smaller bays and inlets. But in the larger world, I was glad to know what spot on earth I occupied, even as I drove away from it. A few days ago, I'd stopped at a new business in town—AgriData, "Bringing precision farming down to earth"—just to see what it was. A young woman explained they provided satellite information and computer software so that, for example, a fertilizer tank moving through a field could automatically vary its concentration from one square yard to another. What would I need to know first as a customer? "Your longitude and latitude," she said matter-of-factly.

One mile into Nelson County I passed a freshly painted sign celebrating the site of the Solberg homestead, the parents' names and dates put up by their children and grandchildren, the open field and tree row a lot like grandfather Charlie's first Montana homestead. Cousin Bill, researching the family's history, drove with his wife Sue to the exact section and quarter and had her take a photograph while he stood as foreground to an enormous flat of sparse grass. Bill is smiling into the camera, because that's what we do, but he also looks uncertain with that space behind him, which is also what we do.

Sometimes we try to track things down, following a mild curiosity or a life's work, and we succeed and fail. I thought of Nicollet working to map a prairie's rivers while aware of their wanderings. On the Missouri, he compared his observations with those of Lewis and Clark, many of the bends they described now unrecognizable and, more, "most probably those determined by us in 1839, and laid down upon my map, will ere long have disappeared."

The Sheyenne River thirty miles ahead of me, I came to McVille—"Large Enough to Serve You, Small Enough to Know You"—crossed Sheyenne Street, and turned down Main, the stores named for their owners: Chuck's Heating and Air Conditioning, Jeannie's Bookkeeping, Joe's Bar, Kathleen's Cut & Curl, Vern's Repair. I stopped for a cup of coffee in the cafe which also held the bowling alley. The town is pronounced *Mack*-Ville because, I'd heard, of the number of families with "Mc" in their last names. I borrowed the phone book and counted them while I sipped my coffee. There were eighty—out of a 559 population—and I mentioned it out loud.

"Oh yes, there's a lot," the waitress-cook said, brushing the back of a hand over her forehead and starting to chop vegetables on a butcher-block. "Not as many as there used to be, of course."

My cup got filled without asking while she talked. Most of the streets were named for early settlers, McDougal, for example, but there was no street named for her uncle. He was the railroad station agent here and then worked double at nearby Kloten. Worked years and years, she emphasized. You'd think they'd have named a street for him. Nothing against the others, you understand. But still you'd think they would have.

A man came in and ordered coffee, saying there was a chance of rain. That couldn't help Devils Lake, I couldn't help but say.

"Devils Lake," he snorted. "They can choke on their water."

"Oh," the woman clucked soothingly, darting me an apologetic glance, "but it's hard on those people that live there."

"That's all right," he said, the way people say it when they don't think something's right. "Years all they thought about was themselves—how they needed this water, that water. So now—" and he picked up his coffee, staring out the window toward the gray elevators, "Sheyenne Valley" painted on their sides.

Turning back to the woman I asked if she was from around here. Well, she was born in Pekin, nearby, and went to school in Tolna, nearby, then left for thirty years and just recently came back. "Thirty years," she repeated, her hand pausing with the knife for a moment before she went back to chopping. "But it hasn't changed that much."

Sliding back behind the wheel, I thought of her curving away from home and returning, stepping back into her own first river, knowing the old people whose last names were streets and the young ones whose first names were stores. There weren't as many as there used to be—true—but it hadn't changed that much.

For a while the road paralleled the Burlington Northern, originally James Hill's Great Northern line in 1906, sliding northwesterly to string together like beads the small towns of Aneta, Kloten, McVille, Pekin, Tolna, Hamar, and Warwick, all spaced seven to ten miles apart so farmers would be within a day's ride of Jim Hill's tracks to deliver grain to town and go back home again. The combined population of all seven was about fifteen hundred but the high-water mark had been only nine hundred more—these had always been small towns. In a few minutes, the land and highway lifted a little so I was looking out and down as I crossed the glacial drift, past "Welcome to Pekin," past "Welcome to Tolna," past a woman's local life. A few more miles and I came to an intermediate destination, the town of Hamar, and turned toward an elevator rising as a landmark.

When Doug Wick's book told me it was named for Hamar, Norway, I'd looked it up in *Prairie Mosaic,* William Sherman's ethnic atlas of North Dakota, and found a lobe of land cross-hatched to indicate a 90 percent Norwegian population, Anglo-Americans the majority to the south, the Sioux to the north. On that map, the ethnic ownership of rectangles became the rounded forms of averages, the map looking like the looping pieces of a jigsaw puzzle or, now that I'd been past the Omlid Slough, an aerial view of the ecosystems of a wetlands habitat.

I drove slowly into town, once sporting a bank, lumberyard, restaurant, telephone office, butcher shop, and funeral home, now few houses occupied, no one in sight, the yards filled with machinery parts, appliances, old boats, and lumber, stored for future use or abandoned, I couldn't tell which. The surviving main street business was the bar, two men standing just outside the door and glancing up at me with a slight widening of their eyes and I had a moment of indecision. It was too early for a beer and I didn't know how to explain my presence anyway. I could ask if he was the bartender who'd found a prehistoric monster in his field, as

Marv had told me in Sheyenne, but I had nothing to say after that. I turned around at the end of the street, passing the bar again, and gave the ritual wave. The men nodded back and I drove past the silent houses again. "Must be lost," I bet one said to the other.

Hamar had seemed lonely and isolated, I thought, retreating to the highway, but such thoughts are too easy. America has always known physical and emotional isolation where the present either echoed the past or waited emptily for the future. Nicollet, passing the Council Bluff area on the Missouri, had looked up at the broken chimneys and scattered masonry of old Fort Atkinson, the first to be built on the Lewis and Clark route, and was struck by its forlorn novelty, "a ruin in the midst of a primitive region still unknown in the history of the world." For that matter, Washington, D.C., was less than forty years old when Nicollet sought governmental support and its wide, grand avenues radiated past mostly vacant lots. "Flattened lonesomeness," Frémont had said of the American capital.

Meanwhile the car hummed on, the sound of tires on the asphalt another kind of American lonesomeness, and I drove past Poplar Grove, which Nicollet had called, translating from the Sioux, the Island of the Woods. Clusters of poplars spread up from layers of glacial outwash so sandy there were wind-shaped dunes, and it was easy to imagine how this particular landscape, depending on the climate and the wind, could move again, like ethnic populations migrating inward and outward, and I coasted by its southern edge.

Only a little later, the Sheyenne five miles south, I made a discovery on my map, a small asterisk labeled "Lookout Mountain." The name seemed like the straight line for a North Dakota joke, but I knew I had to climb it. I wondered how many other states had a Lookout Mountain. Then I wondered how many didn't.

Colorado's Lookout Mountain was from my father's life. A Gray Line driver during his college summers, he rammed an open-roofed, eight-passenger bus up its grade, tourists gasping around the sharp curves as the fenders barely missed one guard post after another. On top was a telescope, the grave of William Cody, a curio shop and museum. Once he drove a group of Indians up and stood by while they gathered around the memorabilia of Buffalo Bill's Wild West Show, pointing out relatives on the gaudy nineteenth-century posters and crying, looking other directions than the abandoned telescope pointed.

Nicollet had his own Lookout Mountain in Tennessee, a view of five states and a point from which he could look down on creeks flowing to the Tennessee River in one direction and the Alabama in another, both eventually joining the Mississippi—looked down, that is, on one of the interlocking pieces of the system he dreamed of mapping completely.

Now mine came into sight, a little hump of grassy hill surrounded by plowed fields. I parked, waded through lush ditch grass and started up, the grass now a wiry bristle under my boots. The hill was a ridge of ground moraine, so I stepped around lichen-covered boulders sledged from Canada by a glacial advance in one millennium and my boots crunched on the gravel of its retreat in another. Coming out on the ridge, I was sorry I'd smiled at the mountain's name. Although only a hundred feet higher than Hamar, whose elevator I could see, it deserved to be called a lookout.

After following the rising and dipping of land along the Sheyenne, Nicollet came to stand on the divide between that basin and the broad plain of the Red River Valley, writing that he never wearied "of seeing a prairie from a hollow or a height" or, as another translated the French, "to look at a prairie up or down." And here I was, looking at a prairie down, the farmland plains stretching six miles to Hamar, six beyond that, maybe six more. The view was so commanding—the military sound of the word not accidental—I was certain others had stood here, Indians, trappers, soldiers, farmers, all climbing this rise to survey the land below and around with a clear eye for game, friends, enemies, or fields.

The day Nicollet overlooked the valley of the Red, he reflected on the differences between the man of the prairies and the man of and mountains. The former "walks only on grass and flowers," nowhere an obstacle, whereas the latter is constantly limited in movement by rocks, trees, torrents, and precipices. The man of the mountains may be victorious in his endeavors, but he is not in command; the man of the prairies is master, free because "nowhere does his eye fall on anything that is not dominated by him." There might be some monotony in "the vast and unvaried view" but, "as one can see all around," there was always the absence of danger.

In my case, I felt no mastery. With no cars on the county roads, no one working in the fields, I was alone in the middle of a high point of air, exposed to the world at large, which did not surround me so much as recede in every direction. I felt in danger of falling into that space, swept bare by the wind, and vanishing. I shifted my feet to break the spell, got my thoughts back to myself, and turned away with a kind of relief. I walked back down across the unimaginable time and space of glacial gravel and massive systems of grass and sat in the car for awhile, letting the image of that huge space fade, then started the car and moved away, Lookout Mountain becoming a minor hill, a rise, a lump on the prairie.

Now I was heading for the Sheyenne to prove Heraclitus wrong, even though I knew he was right. I was a teenager the first time I heard you couldn't step into the same river twice, and—as with "You can't go home again"—experienced a three-thought reaction. The first was quick denial—*of course,* I could—and the second was the realization of the truth, rivers flowing onward in space and home an emotional concept shifting in time; but a third thought could combine the first two, which is the truth of the world, and Heraclitus knew that as well. Although, I'd found out, just as you might not be able to step into the same river twice, you might not be able to read the same Heraclitus twice. Did he say it? We only knew that Plutarch said he did or that Cratylus said Plato said so. And how, exactly, did he say it? Maybe another fragment was more accurate, "As they step into the same river, other and still other waters flow upon them." Yet another version seemed the most paradoxical, and hence the easiest to understand: "We step and do not step into the same rivers." Heraclitus spoke of flux and change, but he also spoke of the unity binding these changes together. Permanence might be a relative term; that everything changed was a half-truth.

I turned left onto a gravel road and, a mile later, turned right. It was harder for Nicollet, of course: 69 days to travel the 1,270 miles up the Missouri from St. Louis to Ft. Pierre, their boat often gone aground or delayed a day or more while they pulled and hacked at logjams clogging their way. Leaving Ft. Pierre on July 1, 1839, the expedition found the river suddenly swollen, a mile and a half wide, taking a day and a half for nineteen men, ten carts, and thirty horses to make it across. By July 3, they were camping and repairing wagons only eight miles away from the fort. On July 17, they crossed the future boundary of North Dakota and in three more days were on the plateau, "surprised and saddened" it brought no relief from the monotony of the scenery. Sincere when he overlooked the Red River Valley and praised the flower-bedecked prairies that aroused the soul most pleasantly, Nicollet also understood those pleasures were temporary compensations for the ennui of the usual unvaried view.

The expedition came through the valley of the James River and, arriving at the *Shayen-oju,* as Nicollet transcribed the local tongue, turned north along its west bank. He found it navigable by canoe, its banks well-wooded, its broad valley possessing fertile soil that offered "many inducements to its settlement." But inducements to travel became fewer. When they moved northward on July 23, a stifling heat covered the land. "We breathe a little on the summits," Nicollet wrote, "but we suffocate in the low places." Hot in the day, the prairie's cool nights brought hordes of mosquitoes so vicious the horses came up to the fires at night to stand in the smoke.

By July 25, twenty miles from the Sheyenne Crossing, they stopped at Lake Jessie and found the water as we find it today, "salty and disagreeable." A year ago I sat in the bar in Binford a few miles west of Jessie, listening to a customer tell what it was like when the lake simply dried up in the '50s—a fine plaster of alkali blown continually through window cracks and under the doors. Now Lake Jessie has swollen back again, all water following the rhythms of flood and drain, swell and subside. Permanence is a relative term.

Hot, tired, thirsty, the expedition moved along the Sheyenne toward the crossing and now I turned off onto the final stretch, the footnote's "unimproved road." I knew I wasn't making this pilgrimage because anything in particular happened there. For

Nicollet, the morning of July 28, around eight o'clock, was just another crossing: "The passage is uneventful, and our horses need only to make strenuous effort to climb up the left bank. The river has been lovely thus far—clear water, rarely less than 70 or 80 feet wide, its bottom pebbly, little mud along its shores, and much fish and game. Woods of oak, white elm, white ash, and a variety of berry bushes, all scarce in these faraway lands."

A windbreak row of pines and cottonwoods on my left, fields of early wheat on my right, I jounced along the ruts of the road, the tires every now and then catching and slowing in the soft sand of glacial outwash, the valley's cut so deep I couldn't see it until, top of a rise, it fell suddenly away below me and I stopped. The first thing that registered—and I was disappointed, wanting to do this alone—was a car parked along the shore and a man fishing below me. The narrow dirt road dove straight down, Nicollet's crossing a fresh concrete ramp on raw boulders piled over a culvert, and then rose straight up again. I got out of the car with my camera.

Upstream, the Sheyenne was a wild little wander down the valley, widening here into a smooth pool, squeezing through a ribbed culvert, and gushing out into another pool before continuing its sinuous glide, the shape hydrologists call a meander after the original Maeander River in Greek Ionia. Moving in its classic loops, it emptied into the Aegean between Ephesus and Miletus where, it so happened, Heraclitus lived. There were other rivers around, of course, but he could have stood on the banks of the Maeander, framing an analogy for the nature of the universe as he watched its moving waters.

Meanwhile, a man was fishing in the river an astronomer turned geographer had crossed. I took my photograph—a dirt road down, a concrete ramp, a dirt road up—and drove down to park beside his car and approach the twenty yards or so where I stood watching his line while asking questions. He was after Northern Pike. There were some good ones here. The crossing was new, all right. A flood took the last one out. Before that, there was a bridge that got flooded out and, before that, another one. Now it depended on what happened in the winter and next spring, he guessed. High water, the ice would go out over the ramp. If not, it'd take it out like all the others. He was sure of that.

Nicollet was not the first to cross here, of course. It was probably the trail of Captain Summers and his two hundred men who'd journeyed up in the summer of 1845 to see what the Indians were doing, and the trail of Captain Burt who, with his own idea of what the Indians were doing, would leave General Sibley's camp in 1863 near Lake Jessie to make a trip to Devils Lake and back and, later, the crossing would be used by mail carriers between Devils Lake and points south. But for me, this was the Nicollet Crossing and at my feet.

Had I meant my pledge literally, "to step in" the same river? Probably, and I thought for a moment of actually struggling down through the tall grasses and wading it. But, I told myself, I would disrupt a man's fishing. Also, the dam of boulders made the upstream side too deep and the downstream side too fast for wading. Also, I would feel very self-conscious. Anyway, I finally told myself, Nicollet was on horseback and didn't actually step into the river himself, even once. The idea itself would have to suffice, the philosophical abstract.

I nodded goodbye to the fisherman, got back in the car and drove slowly across the ramp—crossing the crossing—and up the southern side, my body pressing back in the seat from the steep grade, and then I was on the opposite rim. I took another photograph, although I realized it would be a mirror image of the first, and returned. Maybe Heraclitus was right another time, quoted as saying, "The road up and down is one and the same road." That everything changes was a half-truth. I watched as the fisherman below me stepped back and moved through the tall grass to find another spot.

A weakened Nicollet returned to Washington and what biographer Martha Bray calls the "continued anguish" of working on his map took time, concentration, and perhaps what remained of his health. He had almost eleven thousand astronomical observations to coordinate, but there were also problems with printing the map. Told that it couldn't include his hachure showing topography, he fumed. This was impossible. The map should not just portray "a succession of lakes, marshes, and savannas" but give some evidence of the "hillocks, swells, and uplands," which have a longitudinal and horizontal projection, rather than the simple vertical of a hill. This was what was so striking about that country, he protested.

In early 1843, Congress agreed to publish the map, the scale still too small to give a sense of the texture of the land. "Better than nothing," Nicollet wrote. He was last seen in public during May when he gave a brief reading from his manuscript at the one-hundredth anniversary of the American Philosophical Society. Retiring to a small rooming house, he disappeared into the shadows throughout the warm summer, dying the morning of September 11, 1843, his estate barely able to pay for the funeral, no money for a stone.

Praised in obituaries in Washington, Philadelphia, and Baltimore—he who "measured the distance from star to star," he who "surveyed the majestic works of God"—Nicollet died half a continent away from his former assistant, Frémont, at that moment exploring the Great Salt Lake in Utah. A healthy Nicollet would probably have led this expedition that instead brought Frémont the adulation of his countrymen and made a public aware of the spectacular scenery of the West. The morning of Nicollet's death, Frémont was boiling down five gallons of Great Salt Lake water and analyzing the composition of the resulting fourteen pints of salt, the camp that day at a latitude of 41 15' 50", longitude at 112 06' 43". All I knew was that I was west of the 98th meridian and not yet at the 99th, but that was only from looking at a map someone else had put lines upon. I had no claim on knowing where I was, and I wanted to praise those who did.

Nicollet brought accuracy to a country made inaccurate by a single error. Earlier, Zebulon Pike had miscalculated a Mississippi tributary in Minnesota as 27 minutes too low in latitude. This mistake, accumulating as the distance spread, shrank the maps of that time so there was, as Nicollet wrote, "literally, no room" for the territory he was exploring. He expanded it to its rightful size, the first accurate representation of the Upper Midwest.

"My astronomical observations have, throughout, restored order," Nicollet claimed, which Martha Bray considers "the essence of his work and the pleasure of his life." His accuracy was unusual for the day—"an act of zeal not required of me," he pointed out in his journal. Frémont later said Nicollet set about astronomical observations elaborately fussing with his instruments, preparations similar to those "an Indian makes when he goes where he thinks there are supernatural beings."

Now a satellite in the low heavens, our own version of supernatural beings, beams down information about a field to the farmer who knows his own longitude and latitude, a hard knowledge, and hard won. A hundred fifty years ago, an astronomer moved methodically across the shifting grounds and waters of the prairie and, for this one day, I had traveled the straight lines of highway drawn across the ebb and flow of everything else. Currents had left the landscape configured in swirl and eddy, the country filling up and draining away like the indefinite territories of grassland or the seasonal nation-states of pools in a wetlands marsh.

I looked back from the car. Below me, other and still other waters moved under the new concrete ramp—a bridge permanent until next year's waters. In the valley bottom, the fisherman once more moved away from the bank into the tall marsh grass and then forward to cast his line. In less than a minute, he backed up and came near another spot to cast. And then again, trying and retrying his luck. He looked as if he could do that forever, retreating from the river and approaching it, over and over.

lost in the bottomlands

"You don't know what it's like," my daughter Lynn said on the drive back from rescuing me out of the tangles of the Sheyenne bottomlands, "to watch your father, almost sixty, disappear around a bend in a canoe heading off to God knows where." And I didn't know, not having thought I was almost sixty—until then—and certain I knew, along with God, exactly where I was heading.

The main worry I had that late June about canoeing and camping a stretch of the Sheyenne the last few miles of Nelson County and halfway through Griggs was that it was too commonplace. I wouldn't be Samuel Clemens following life on the Mississippi and I wouldn't be John Neihardt following the symbol of his soul, the Missouri, in 1909. I would not even be Thoreau setting forth with his brother John on the Concord and Merrimac Rivers in 1839—in August, a month after Nicollet crossed the Sheyenne heading toward Devils Lake—to see what country lay behind him.

The Sheyenne wound so narrowly through pastures and fields that I might be trespassing and I imagined a county sheriff coming upon my bedroll tucked into the small space between the stream and a private fence. Or if not illegal, then laughable, a solitary gray-haired figure, a new Rip Van Winkle, paddling past farmers working the fields or sitting on their back porches. I was, therefore, both afraid and embarrassed to ask for advice.

I wasn't worried about the canoeing—it seemed simple to put in south of McVille and let the slow current take me thirty miles or so downstream to Sibley's Crossing where the Sheyenne backs up at the beginning of Lake Ashtabula. I knew the river meandered—a friend suggested three miles of water to one mile of map—but I had three or four days to spare. Nicollet had declared the Sheyenne passable by canoe and I'd checked some country road crossings, the river flowing openly around a bend and disappearing openly around the next. There was nothing to worry about. What did I know.

Lynn was picking me up after work that Wednesday outside my apartment building, the Red River dozing its way north just beyond the parking lot, and I waited in the lobby hung with photographs of steamboats from the years of crowded river traffic. None of them large—200 feet or less—they often trailed long barges behind them, hauling farm equipment, flour, supplies, and lumber downstream to Fort Garry, the original Winnipeg, and then back to the upstream terminal of Fargo-Moorhead, huge loads of furs at first, brimming bushels of wheat later.

One of the photos showed the first steamboat on the river, the *Anson Northrup*, built in 1859. Perhaps it wasn't very well built as it sank a few years later near Winnipeg but it looked impressive to me each day as I came off the elevator. Last winter I'd read Roy Johnson's account of steamboating on the Red with its "long and colorful history," and I guessed that fifty years—the *Grand Forks* took its final trip in 1909, two years after my mother's birth in Westhope—qualified as long compared to the short lifetimes of forts or towns betting wrong on the railroad's direction. But colorful, it certainly was. Johnson nicely describes those days, boats "bulging with enormous cargoes" and loaded with salesmen and scientists, speculators and homesteaders, government officials and Mennonites from Russia—steaming past towns, shipyards, and docks, hotels and warehouses and saloons, and flour mills and cafes, and more for fifty years' worth. But for me that time was a series of sepia-tinged photographs on the wall of a remodeled hotel where senior citizens sat in the lobby. Or almost senior citizens.

Two years after I left Dakota, a winter of heavy snow and a terrible spring melt brought the Red to rise easily over my parking lot to become the great Grand Forks Flood and I, in another state by that time, watched the local news made national, houses overwhelmed, the city's center part of the river's middle, two blocks of buildings blazing as helplessly as a homesteader's barn in a prairie fire. And I would think of my lobby inundated, the *Anson Northrup* washed from its moorings on the wall and riding the trashy currents of disaster.

But the day was dry and warm when Lynn arrived in her van, the 18-foot aluminum Grumman lashed on top. She watched, half encouraging, half dubious, as I loaded my gear into the van, sleeping bag, tent, water, backpack, and one-burner propane stove. I also had—because I'd found it in my toolbox—a small pruning-saw in case there might be a branch across the river.

We turned south at McVille, slipped into the Sheyenne Valley, and stopped at a bridge. The river looked open but Lynn suggested checking around that curve and we found the Sheyenne gurgling through a tangle of branches from two downed trees blocking anything like a canoe. Lynn looked at me. All right, I shrugged, there was another crossing two miles down. That would save me two miles. Even better, I told her.

At that bridge, we checked beyond the first bend and found it clear. This was fine. Lynn shook her head. We unloaded the canoe and I yanked it through the grass, stowed my gear and stepped in. I'd probably camp tonight on the other side of the next county bridge. She should pick me up at five o'clock Saturday afternoon at the cafe at Sibley, okay? And don't worry about being late. If I got there earlier, it'd be easy to while away the time. I settled in and pushed off but Lynn wanted to take a picture so I posed in mid-stream, paddle lifted, then turned and dug in. She took one more photo—which I didn't know until later—the back of her father, almost sixty, disappearing around the bend, heading toward God alone knew where.

Rivers, for Thoreau, were "the constant lure to distant enterprise and adventure" and "the natural highways of all nations" but the Sheyenne had not been a highway for much of anything and I was not being lured to enterprise or adventure. In neutral country for awhile, halfway between the Sioux reservation and the Cheyenne's ancient village, between Nicollet's crossing upstream and General Sibley's downstream, I expected nothing on either hand to remind me of history as I floated through a familiar landscape, a century of farmers.

I was lured to find the river's movement, the "lapse of the current," which Thoreau took as "an emblem of all progress, following the same law with the same system, with time, and all that is made," believing, along with other mid-nineteenth-century Transcendentalists, that Nature was a set of spiritual hieroglyphics. I'd thought something like that and although I wasn't sure I agreed with Emerson that "Nature is the symbol of spirit" or that "Particular natural facts are symbols of particular spiritual facts," I thought there was some connection.

Thoreau was also fascinated with the natural scientist Louis Agassiz—his name later given to the ice age lake on whose fertile bottom now sat Grand Forks—who advised his students to study and trust Nature, rather than books, as the objective giver of truth. "No one can warp her to suit his own views," he declared as he presented "lessons of God's magnificence" drawn from his study of marine invertebrates, each natural object "a thought of God." But even if no such transcendental connection actually existed, it often *felt* that way and that was enough for me. Whether I'd discover a liquid progress or find some other emblem, I'd let the current lapse me along and see what I found in drifting.

It was still sunny, the tall grasses along the shore bowing over to complete the circle with their bowed up reflections. I paddled around an occasional bare log anchored in the flow. Here and there cattle had gathered, the mud pocked into the shapes of their hooves. The stream ran smoothly.

Emerson described setting out for a boating experience with Thoreau, crossing only one local field to leave time, science, and history behind, whereupon they "entered into Nature with one stroke of a paddle." In about fifteen minutes, I came around a bend and entered into Nature myself, coming suddenly upon a ten-foot high, bank-to-bank log-jam, two or three trees having fallen into and across the river, capturing flood-driven branches and debris. I back-paddled fiercely but the stream pulled me on, the bow hitting the first log and stopping with a shudder, the current bringing the stern around, smacking me flat against the jam. I yanked at branches, the canoe trembling and rocking, but they resisted, the lifts and falls of the river over time having woven together a knotted witch's nest of logs and sticks, and I made only a few toothy scratches with my pruning saw before I gave up. With a few heaves, I back-paddled the canoe, then dug fiercely to the right to put ashore. "Well," I may have said out loud as I stood on the bank.

It took two trips to portage, one to lug the gear and one to pull the canoe through the long grass, and I put back in. Midstream, I gave a few vigorous strokes, the water hissing beneath me as I lurched forward. That wasn't so bad, I told myself. It hadn't taken that long. Ten minutes later, around another bend, I found another logjam, as large and complete an obstruction as the first one. "Well," I may have said out loud again, with a slightly different tone.

The idealist minister Henry Van Dyke proclaimed, in his 1901 *Little Rivers,* that "every river that flows is good, and has something worthy to be loved." I agreed with that and, yes, a river was probably "the most human and companionable of all inanimate things," full of character and life and good fellowship, but that early evening I grew less sure of the Sheyenne's character and doubted its fellowship completely. I had paddled for ten minutes and spent fifteen portaging around a log-jam to put in and paddle ten minutes until the next one.

I hadn't understood my view from bridges was a false one, the river having been straightened, log-jams removed to protect the bridge. Out of sight of the road, it was a series of tight twistings blocked with accumulated debris. And I hadn't expected the level of land to change. Sometimes I glided abreast of a low pasture but most of the time I was enclosed by high banks. The valley was over half a mile wide and a hundred feet deep but I was a dozen feet farther down in an incised stream, out of sight, at the bottom of the bottom.

I had little company. Coming around a bend I did see a beaver cutting a V across the water who quickly disappeared with a whack of his tail, and once a heron rose in front of me and flapped almost mournfully on, following the river's course to disappear, but nothing else. There were, of course, trees—mostly elm and oak—and tall grasses along the river, which made it at least a strip of semi-wildness but there was something almost foreboding about the river and its banks.

Nor was I in the middle of a settled countryside. Once I passed a wooden wagon wheel half-sunken in the mud along the shore, its bone-white spokes flaking away, its loose, rusted iron rim quivering in the current. Another time, the land falling a bit so I could see, a white farmhouse appeared ahead in the trees and I straightened up. As I came closer, however, it turned into a weathered frame house starting to tilt, its back door missing, a trailer with broken windows behind it, a double abandonment.

After the heron, there'd been no animal life and after the deserted house and trailer no signs of humanity, not even the echo of a car or tractor in the distance. Nothing was happening around me, although I moved through evidence of happenings, passing the mud-caked skeleton of a tree, its intricate root-system exposed as if an anatomy lesson, and then clutches of straw plastered in branches six feet above the ground by spring floods. I was exploring, in a sense. But it felt more as if I had disappeared, dropped off the end of the earth. I was very much alone and it was getting dark. By nine o'clock, tired from six portages in three hours—I'd kept count—and concerned about the clouds building up, I pulled ashore and unloaded my gear. Snapping the tent up, I boiled water for instant coffee, then drank it while I heated up stew and munched on dry crackers in the otherwise absolute silence.

On my township map, the river wound gently through squared-off sections but my topographical map showed a torturous course, the river turning east, north, south, west, the banks of the valley swirling with elevation lines, the scratches of Nature's ups and downs. I didn't know exactly where I was on either map, but my first landmark, the bridge, had not been reached so I hadn't gone three land miles. I decided I'd think better in the morning and slid into my sleeping-bag. My legs ached a little from the portages and I stretched them out fiercely and let them relax. The ground felt hard at first and then softened as I drifted into sleep. Around midnight I woke to the steady ticking of rain on the tent, but I was dry, I was fine, I was going back to sleep, and I didn't even wonder what Lynn might be thinking if she were lying awake.

On the last of August in 1839, Nicollet returned from his Dakota journey, entering the "familiar country" of Minnesota, the same day Thoreau and his older brother John began their tour that would become *A Week on the Concord and Merrimac Rivers,* a kind of "sacerdotal withdrawal from the village," Thoreau suggested, leaving a familiar country to discover the surviving wilderness of New England. One hundred fifty-six years and two months later, I woke up on the banks of the Sheyenne after a night of insistent rain.

Water had collected from some small leak, soaking the bottom half of my sleeping bag, and I crawled out of the tent, the trees dripping, the long grasses slippery, the whole country having wept, as Thoreau described a morning on his river. For him, a sparrow had trilled in the dismal dampness with a "cheery faith" but I heard no such spiritual messenger and quickly drank a cup of coffee, ate a fruit bar, struck a wet camp, and, soaked, settled myself in the canoe. I pushed off with a stroke, the water hissing under my aluminum shell, and settled in again.

Here and there thick chocolate rivulets tumbled into the river from the torn pasture land, a stream clear and pebble-bottomed to earlier explorers now the recipient of an eroding usefulness. The silty gurgle from the fields and the trapped deadfalls made it seem I was traveling a series of disasters, but I tried to concentrate on the flow of the water. Thoreau said that drifting downstream favored a meditative state as one yielded to "the liquid undulating lapse of thought"—and thus I lapsed on. If the river followed the same law as everything else, what was that law? It turned out that seeing a river as an emblem of uniform progress was a little too simple.

There's a rhythm to meandering streams, a combination of the movement of water both between banks and within itself. Given a river of a certain length left to natural processes, a meander will result because water is a random object.

"Water is a *random object*?" I asked Frank Beaver as we sat in his university office a month later. I was trying to find out exactly what I'd experienced.

"Well, sure," Frank said. "Water can't resist any stress so anything that happens is going to cause movement. Say we have a straight river." He drew two parallel red lines and a third winding between them. "It will often develop a sinuous thalweg and that can lead to—"

"A thalweg?"

"That's if you connect the deepest points of a stream channel with a line."

"And this is in a meander?"

"It's anywhere," he shrugged, pulling my attention back to his drawing. "If you have a stream with straight banks the thalweg is still going to wind from side to side inside the water. This lifts the water surface slightly against one bank, eroding more on that side than the other."

I watched the red lines thicken on Frank's sheet of paper, small arrows surfacing and bending as he spoke. The water starts to curve, okay? So it pushes faster, erodes more of the cut-bank— scratch, scratch with the red pen—and on the inside of the curve— scratch, scratch—the water slows down so it deposits sand and silt and forms the point-bar, okay?

Now, do I know laminar flow from turbulent flow? Well, if you have a straight channel of slow water, the layers are parallel, shearing over each other, and that's laminar flow. The maximum velocity in the stream is in the middle, just below the surface because the friction of the stream-bed slows the lower part and the friction of the banks the outer part. But when you get going faster— Frank turned the paper over, more red lines, curving arrows— you start to get turbulent flow, secondary eddies superimposing themselves on the main forward one. And now we've got just one more step. Water flows primarily downstream because water's an expression of gravity.

"Water's an *expression*?" I interrupted, lifting my eyebrows.

"Of gravity," Frank nodded, not lifting his.

So. Here was water moving primarily downstream, laminar and turbulent, but there was another flow, and the red pen scratched some more. Surface water moves in toward the center of the stream and down, while bottom water moves outward and up which produces a helical movement of the whole mass, a spiral energy that could really help create meandering from side to side, the ultimate cause of which is the sinuous nature of water itself, Frank ended, re-capping his red pen and shoving the boiling tubular diagrams of the inside of a river across his flat desk. "It's the way water works," he said.

On the Sheyenne that day, I was feeling what I couldn't yet explain. Van Dyke had observed that his little companionable rivers molded the shore as the shore molded them like the union of soul and body. I knew what that meant—the origin of "river" being the Latin *ripa* for bank, the movement defined by its limitations—but I hadn't thought about being at the mercy of both shore and stream, of the helical flow or even so obvious a feature as cut-banks and point-bars. If water was an expression of gravity, the course of my canoe was an expression of water and I was helpless in a push of invisible dynamics. All I could do was guide the canoe into the current, following the faster, deeper water to the left and then ricocheting to the right around the next knot of land.

Trapped in the current that shaped the bank, I was also trapped by barriers intruding from the shore. The first log jam and portage for Thursday came in twenty minutes. I slipped and slid through rain-slick bushes, occasionally stumbling over fallen trunks hidden in the grass, dragging the muddy canoe under low, snagging branches and over hummocks of soaked grass. By the time I pushed off again, I was breathing heavily, my boots and pants shiny with water and mud.

It took about fifteen minutes of paddling to reach the next log-jam and a heart-breaking portage. The current was too fast to turn back into the shallows and the banks so high I had to toss a rope up around a tree and pull first myself up and then the canoe. I slithered it across the grass to an open space, looked down-stream and saw another log-jam, waded through hip-high grass for twenty yards around a bend to another. By this time I had stopped talking out loud—I didn't want to hear it. I went back, portaging around all three by hauling the canoe straight inland because the Sheyenne, the helical flow of an element unable to withstand any stress, was coming back at me from the opposite direction.

Portaging around the thick jams had taken on a dogged, des-perate quality so that when I actually made it through one I was unduly pleased. At one jam I found a large branch that, removed by my saw, allowed an opening. The next consisted of a half-submerged log running the width of the river, another fully branched tree having fallen over it. Hoping that without my weight the buoyant canoe might slide over the log, I rammed the prow for-ward, grabbed the suspended branches of the second tree and lifted myself so the canoe bobbed up and over the log. I imagined what it might look like if I missed, dangling in the middle of the stream while my supplies sailed safely on, but I managed to catch it with my boots and slide back down.

Soon I was again in the bottom of a steep ditch between banks of weathered shale and siltstone, sediment settling just off-shore the ancient ocean-way of North America now an exposed wall of loose gray bits which, when I brushed them in passing, flaked easily away into the water with a spattering hiss. The point-bars were made of the same shale, popcorn-sized chips of gray and black, whose looks were deceiving. Once I nosed in and stepped out on the solid crusty flakes to look around and another time stepped out with one foot and sank to my knee in shale-covered mud.

At about ten o'clock I hit the county bridge I'd been expecting last night and pulled up on the rocks underneath to make a cup of coffee. The desolate silence—not a farmhouse seen, nothing heard all morning—was broken suddenly when a car passed overhead, the bridge resounding loudly, and I felt almost cheerful near civilization again. I even felt a little good humor at being hidden from sight and society under the pilings of the bridge while a citizen rumbled on his way, never suspecting my way, a drifter, literally.

By the time I finished my coffee, the sun had come out and around the next broad bend I slid into a stretch of pastoral stream, a painting in which water mirrored its shoreline trees. It was not Thoreau's New England air and water, so transparent that "we are uncertain whether the water floated the land, or the land held the water in its bosom," but it was a Dakota version, the river darkly the river, the tan reflections of trees and grasses blending in a murky harmony. The banks lowered and fell back so that I could actually see some of the surrounding countryside—elms, a knobby pasture—then rose again like walls and I focused once more on the opaque, grainy flow.

Here and there the end of a branch stuck up, the brown water dividing into a set of V-shaped ripples before it joined seamlessly together again. Sometimes a jutting stick would bob helplessly insistent, pushed forward by the current to its point of tension and snapping back, an incessant nodding at forces beyond its control. So this was eternal law, an emblem of endurance or futility or both at once, nature assimilating all the contrasts and distinctions which we worry out and worry about.

Around noon and after several more portages, I had a respite of lunch and coffee on the tip of a point-bar, but after that it was river and log-jam, paddle and portage, until mid-afternoon when— muddy, still wet, arms and legs a little rubbery—I came to another wall of wedged driftwood beside a collapsed barn and deteriorating trailer. Checking downstream, I counted three log-jams in the next half-mile and came back, intent on surrender. I would simply walk up the hill and find help. George Catlin, the western and plains artist, often landed his skiff and "mounted the green carpeted bluffs, whose soft grassy tops invited me to recline, where I was at once lost in contemplation" but the view from my bluff was different. I could see at least four miles in each direction but, except for a herd of cows, saw nothing, no barn, no house, no road. I thought of simply starting to walk—I'd have to reach a house sometime—but that wouldn't solve the problem of getting the canoe out. I was trapped with it. I stood there for a long time, turning around as if expecting something to change. "One must needs climb a hill to know what world he inhabits," Thoreau wrote one century and sixteen days before I was born, and I had climbed one but couldn't believe it was my world, this empty a landscape this close to home. I sighed an exasperated puff of air, then started back down.

I lugged my gear the half mile downstream, scaring up a deer who bounded with a certain difficulty herself under low-hanging branches and over fallen trees, then tramped back to haul the canoe ahead. Putting in, I paddled and hit another log-jam, portaged, paddled and hit another one, until dark. Camp that night was a small peninsula, the Sheyenne in front of me moving south, the Sheyenne behind me moving north. Just as I finished heating water, it started to rain again and I had hot instant coffee and cold stew in my tent.

That Thursday night I gave myself a speech, needing the words out loud in the air. It was a kind of adventure, true. I was tired of this adventure, very true. There was no way of knowing where I would be Saturday afternoon except that it would *not* be Sibley. I had to quit. The only thing to do tomorrow was to push on and get out of the river at the first house I saw. I warned myself not to think that if I hit an easy stretch it would be all right because it wouldn't be all right for long. Remember that, I told myself. Promise me.

I lay back, surrender bringing its own relief. The rain had stopped tapping against the tent and the bottomland was silent. One of the many things I didn't know in the dark end of that Thursday was that down river a few miles, just off the Sheyenne near Cooperstown, four men had been digging and brushing to uncover the backbone, ribs, and breastbone of a platycarpus, an almost thirty-foot-long creature with a long toothy snout and scaly skin, the main predator of the ancient sea that had covered the bottomlands 75 million years ago. Reading about the fossil later, I remembered the one sound I'd heard in the darkness.

It was after midnight when a huge, echoing, two-part ka-thunk of a splash a few yards away brought me upright, body tingling with adrenaline. I waited, my heart thumping, but nothing else happened. A beaver? Some large fish? If so, the size of a platycarpus. I lay back down and listened to my heart gradually slow. Something was "out there," as we sometimes say of nature, something was large and hidden inside the mystery of the dark water that kept rolling in and over upon itself, cutting to one side, lying down to the other.

The next morning's bright sunshine—"The sun is new every day," Aristotle said Heraclitus said—and my decision to quit whenever I could combined to lighten my heart. I took my time at breakfast, washed in the river, and lounged around over a cup of coffee, drying out a bit. I pulled the canoe up, dragged it through my campsite and slid it back in the river heading the opposite direction, putting off about eight o'clock. You're out the first chance you get, I reminded myself.

Two or three tiring portages later, about mid-morning, I came around a steep-walled bend to find more deadwood tangle. Pulling myself up the muddy bank by the roots of trees, I saw, almost all the way up on the ridge of the Sheyenne Valley, a heavenly white farmhouse with a trimmed lawn. I tied the canoe to one of the roots and headed up the steep cattle path to the house.

Mr. Hengsa, the Norwegian farmer who came out on the porch, was surely surprised to see a muddy, disheveled stranger emerge from the bottomlands but his face was neutrally polite. I needed to use his phone, I explained. I'd been trying to canoe the Sheyenne and there were too many log-jams. Oh, he knew what I meant. His two nephews had tried it—took them three hours to go two miles to the church down by the bridge. That outbreak of Dutch elm disease in the mid '80s, you know. That was what killed a lot of the Sheyenne elm and caused so much driftwood.

Well, come on in, and he introduced his mother who offered coffee and "bars," a crusty fruit staple in this part of the country. I accepted, then called Lynn at work, repeating the directions as the Hengsas gave them—west one mile, south two miles, and so on.

I had a second coffee and two more bars. Did I want to wait inside? No, but thanks. I had to haul the canoe up and I was too muddy anyway. I'd just wait out in their yard. Mr. Hengsa followed me out onto the porch and we stood looking down to the Sheyenne, which had, from this perspective, sunken back into mere decoration, a lovely hump of trees meandering in the lush valley.

"It's pretty here," I finally said.

"That's what they say," he replied. When I glanced at him, he shrugged. "I mean, I've lived here all my life."

I nodded, though I wasn't sure what I was agreeing to. He went back in and I stood looking down a while longer. "Vista"—and that's what the valley was at that moment—suggests a physical as well as a mental view, the way we lived upon the earth teaching us how to live inside ourselves. The ancient Indo-European *weid* is at the root of the multiple words we use for "seeing"—of vista and view, vision and advice, wit, wisdom, and evidence and even of idea itself. I stared at the broad overview of pleasantly wooded curves, a curtain draped over the reality of what it was like to be inside of them. It would be easier to discover another New World, Thoreau thought, "than to go within one fold of this which we appear to know so well." I'd been isolated in the heart of my own countryside, now at home in a stranger's side yard, but at least I'd tried to go within one such fold. I'd wanted to find a drift of thought, a union of body and soul and the outside world, and I'd ridden the surface of laminar, turbulent and helical flow, as passive as water myself, pulled by gravity, that singular law which causes a million expressive complications every second in a small Dakota river.

Then I went back down, unloaded my gear and lugged it up the slippery cattle path to the barn, catching my breath, and then on up to a horse trailer beside the gravel driveway. Hauling the canoe up the steep slope took almost half an hour, a few yards at a time before I had to rest, but it was the last thing I'd have to do today, I told myself. I sprawled against the horse trailer, physically stunned by the effort of the last few days and the relief from the effort, relaxing into a tired meditation and watching fluttering white cabbage moths. Their jagged flight followed the slope of the grass but when they hit the trees across the driveway at the edge of the lawn, they rose immediately—almost breathtakingly for such small creature—until they were the same distance above the trees as they had been from the grass. I vaguely wondered what their vista was.

Emerson would have proclaimed them a lesson, Agassiz a number of God's little thoughts. Fragments of lacy white fluttering around me, I lay in a stunned reverie, the outer world one with my inner, until a pickup clattered past on the gravel drive and I opened my eyes. Mr. Hengsa, on his way somewhere, waved. I, no longer on my way anywhere, waved back.

following general sibley

"America's not going to last," my gray-haired lunch companion at the Aneta cafe snapped, sitting back and finishing
his coffee. "Too many problems."

"What would make it better?" I asked.

He leaned forward again. "If those militia groups would
just get together and take over."

Aneta, Queen City of the Upper Sheyenne, about five
miles east of the river, is a nice little town, notwithstanding
one dark-minded citizen. It had shrunk from five hundred
in the '40s to three hundred now, the erosion of four people
a year, a couple hundred nearby farms "lost," the remaining
farms growing a couple hundred acres each.

I'd been through town several times that mid-summer tracking General Henry H. Sibley's trail along and across the Sheyenne. The ruler of a Minnesota hunting lodge that housed Nicollet on his trip through and the state's first governor from 1858–1860, Sibley had brought what was called "order" to Minnesota after the uprising and, in 1863, followed the Sioux into Dakota, although how many were guilty or innocent, one could wonder about and never know. Those weeks following a trail of war disoriented me in several ways and today it was thanks to the citizen who stopped by my table with a cup of coffee just as I lifted my hamburger from a nest of searingly fresh French fries. Did I mind if he sat down?

Immediately: What did I think about universities getting more leftist? I didn't know they had. Oh? Hadn't I heard about this professor saying spanking children hurt their personalities? He gave a quick, harsh laugh and I remembered the Rush Limbaugh radio show had probably ended at noon. Listen, he leaned forward. Let me tell you. Three girls came in here the other day from the college down at Valley City and were giving *classes* for mothers about feeding babies. When I stared, he went on scornfully. Look, do you know how to feed babies? Like this, he said, clapping both hands to one bony breast so fiercely I winced. That's all you need to know about feeding babies, he scoffed with another sip of coffee. I took a bite of my hamburger. And did I know what was happening in Texas?

See, he had a retirement place down there in a trailer court, but it got sold five years ago to "two Hispanic businessmen" and now there were only a dozen or so "white people" left.

There was more and he told me more as I ate faster and finally finished, leaving with the dire echo of his solution.

∽

Sibley's march—and, elsewhere in North Dakota, General Sully's—
came at a time in our history when something like militia groups
did try to take over the countryside, small but important treks
now evidenced by important but small markers scattered along
the road. I thought many things about tracing the march, necessary only because I wanted to follow the Sheyenne, and I had been
wrong, time after time.

At the beginning I thought the past and present were separate, but my travel wavered between both. I thought the language
in which battles were written would make no difference to me but
I was almost smothered by its rhetoric of righteousness. At the
beginning I thought the matter either simple or complicated, depending on how closely you looked, but I was wrong again. It was
both at once, epic and pathetic, and I never found a perspective to
make it easier to view. It was a more than strange time for me,
advancing out from my Grand Forks apartment to scout around
and then retreat, enlightened and confused, a remote visitor in
some way implicated, to some degree responsible.

At the beginning I did not, incredibly enough, think of the
racial issues involved, not connecting my mother's fear in the
stranded Dodge as two Indians emerged from the Montana woods
to circle the car and leave with my lunch companion's loss of his
white trailer court in Texas. It was difficult for me to connect the
current year with, for example, 1910, but it turned out to be important to do just that.

That was the date Henry Pratt Fairchild had picked as a piv-
otal national moment in his mid-twenties book, *The Melting-Pot
Mistake*. Since the 1880s, immigrants had arrived from southern
and eastern Europe rather than northern and no melting pot could
fuse *this* variety—the "specialization" of the English-Nordic type
would be lost if not somehow protected. Because we'd developed

an American culture by 1910, as Fairchild figured it, the racial composite that year was "largely responsible" for that endeavor, so he proposed that immigration be set at 3 percent of a nationality's numbers in 1910.

By the time the idea got through Congress, it had changed to flat limits based on the population of 1920—when an American culture, one supposes, was even more developed. It would take a long time for us to realize that the first immigrant English were pretty much like the Irish, Germans, and Scandinavians who followed them who were pretty much like the Italians, Jews, and Poles who followed them. Maybe, considering my fellow citizen in the cafe, it will take us another long time.

Of course, one could argue for keeping the national composition as it was when the Declaration of Independence was signed but we wouldn't have dreamed of including the Americans already born on this floating continent for centuries, the "red devils," according to many newspapers and much common talk, who should be exterminated.

The White Answer to the Indian Question was based on an inseparable combination of race and real estate. Charles Bryant, writing a couple of years after the Minnesota massacre, asserted the Great Law of Right: God had ordered man to "subdue" the earth and the Indian had obviously refused. This was not a new thought—a 1652 Massachusetts court said land could belong to Indians, according to Genesis, "by subduing of same"—but Bryant brutally spelled it out: "On the one side stood the white race in the command of God, armed with his law; on the other, the savage, resisting the execution of that law," the Indians, therefore, "in the wrongful possession of a continent required by the superior right of the white man." God, in other words, made us do it. And the earth around here began to be subdued.

The plan, a year after the 1862 Uprising, was for Sibley to march northwest from Minnesota's Fort Ridgely and follow the Sheyenne to where the hostiles had presumably wintered at Devils Lake, and for Sully to come up the Missouri to Devils Lake from the southwest. Sully didn't arrive in time and Sibley, after three events called battles, pushed some Sioux across the Missouri and marched back home. This was the first decisive defeat of the Plains Indians, it was said. This only fanned the flames of war more fiercely, it was said. True. All true.

Moving ten to fifteen miles a day, the expedition took two months, two weeks, and four days to travel more than a thousand miles into and back out of Dakota. Last winter, I'd followed the major little war in the diaries of Col. William Marshal and soldier Enoch Eastman, Nathaniel West's 1889 book on Sibley, Oscar Wall's reminiscence in 1909, and the mid-1920s account of historian Dana Wright. Now I was following them over the earth, and I drove south to meet the general coming north.

The departure from Fort Ridgely was, for Wall, "one of the grandest military pageants ever witnessed in Minnesota," a column stretching six miles, more than 340 wagons hauled by a thousand animals followed by several hundred head of beef cattle, the eight hundred horses of the cavalry, the fifty of the artillery, and about four thousand men. But pageantry quickly gave way to a burning Dakota summer. For Nathaniel West it was a journey "through solitudes, sandhills and bluffs, streams stagnant or covered with scum, ridges loaded with boulders, prairies blasted by fire." To the hot suns and fierce thunderstorms he added, in an Old Testament vein, "grasshoppers thick as the locusts of Egypt and filling the air like snowflakes; huge flies obedient to Beelzebub, and, by the billion, drawing the blood from mules, horses and men."

With temperatures around 100°F and little rain, the earth split open beneath hooves and feet and wheel rims and stirred into suffocating dust. On July 2, the expedition crossed the future boundary of North Dakota near Skunk Lake, a mile long, half-mile wide shine of water Nicollet had noted on his map of 1839. It was brackish enough—both whites and Indians called it Skunk—but, compared to what they'd been through, it seemed an inviting place to camp and rest.

In my own July, I arrived to find Skunk Lake renamed Tewaukon, "Spirit Lodge," the area now a National Wildlife Refuge. A large plaque outside the visitor center commemorated John Langie, a *metis*—French and Indian—who'd served as scout for Sibley and returned ten years later, the first grower of hard red spring wheat in Sargent County. The plaque quoted an 1883 county newspaper: "John Lonjay [*sic*] and his wife were in Linton to trade. He drives a good team, is honest, industrious, and makes money farming."

I walked up the road to the small family cemetery at the edge of the lake and stood at Langie's stone, a good farmer who had subdued the earth for a while. Other stones were for the LaBelles, the family John's daughter married into, her husband Louis a Sisseton Sioux, the first elected sheriff for the reservation just south of the lake. It was a land we'd fought hard to own, first in war and then against weather for the sake of God and America and agriculture. Now, as a wildlife refuge, we gave it back, old farms that shouldn't have been farms in the first place or were no longer needed, fenced fields blurring into a half-imaginary wilderness.

Langie was born in 1839 and died in 1906—the year the railroad moved on from Aneta to Devils Lake, a few years before

Fairchild's missed moment to freeze the percentages of immigration—a native-born alien in America who lived a life across two centuries and two races. As I stood in the small cemetery the wind started to rustle the lakeshore grass, but for a moment I thought the world was as quiet as I'd ever heard it.

The July sun burned in the 90s as I walked back toward the visitor center and my car. After toiling over hell's parched ground through suffocating dust, Sibley's soldiers bathed and fished in these shallows, some of the officers rigging a raft with sails, tacking back and forth in the breeze. On my way out, wanting to feel I'd been here, I stopped, walked down to the shore and knelt. Swirling away clumps of greenish-yellow scum and duckweed, I cupped both hands down and brought them to my face, a refreshing swash of cold that surprised me, as if I'd been dreaming. I slid back into my car, face still wet, and started north.

Sibley's First Crossing of the Sheyenne was near the Cheyenne village I'd visit in a few weeks so I headed for the Second and his namesake town, turning north through Lisbon, crossing the Sheyenne, a mild pastoral stream on the northern edge. I'd drive one hundred fifty miles and make it by lunch. It took Sibley fourteen days.

The expedition usually roused at two or three in the morning, had breakfast by four, and tried to camp by noon to avoid the worst heat. The morning of July 3 as they left Skunk Lake, the air, said Marshall, was "like the blast of a furnace." Grasshoppers had stripped whatever hadn't burned so the men continued through choking clouds of dust. The line of march frayed at the ends and broke in the middle, cattle and horses strung out so loosely they were left behind to be re-captured later, many of the men falling out, straggling exhausted into the camp, near present day Milnor, later and later that evening.

The morning of July 4, they set up Camp Hayes near Lisbon, hoisting a flag on a tall pole of white ash and giving a 39-gun salute to honor the states and territories, a national festivity in what must have seemed the heart of nothingness. Beyond the buffalo herds browsing leisurely in every direction, Oscar Wall wrote, "nothing was seen but arched skies and boundless plains" and he noted how far they were from the traditional setting, no citizens in carriages, no best girl, red lemonade, brass band, shady grove. "How painfully absent" these things seemed, he wrote, "how eloquently silent."

Enoch Eastman noted in his diary only that the band played and some of the men carried Colonel Crook around camp on their shoulders before he gave a short speech Enoch couldn't hear. According to Col. Marshall, the officers shared a fruit cake Mrs. Sibley had sent along, received the General's thanks for their confidence, and were assured they would not turn back until Little Crow and his fellow murderers had been killed. Actually, Little Crow had been shot the day before picking berries with his son near Hutchinson, Minnesota, and by the time Sibley heard the news Little Crow's scalp was on display at the historical rooms in the state capital, having netted someone the $25 reward.

After resting a week, they moved on. The flag pole was finally shattered by lightning, then cut down in the winter of 1891 for firewood. Later, the commander of the Grand Army of the Republic post at Abercrombie had the stump dug up and made into gavels, which were given to various GAR posts, one kind of historical remembrance. But there were others less accurate. When surveyors, twenty years later, discovered the litter of scraps, boot heels, shoes, buttons, and bullets, they recorded it as a battle site, a confusion continuing for years in North Dakota along the army's route. Settlers easily mistook the low sod bulwarks Sibley ordered thrown up at almost every camp as signs of battle. More dramatically, because the cooking fires were laid in narrow trenches, the old campsites were marked by grassy sinks looking like nothing so much as forgotten graves. Thus were things left behind and lost, or found and honored, or mistaken for something else.

The journey had become monotonous—"the history of one day," Sibley wrote to his wife, "is the record of another, and I assure you there is a tiresome sameness about these vast prairies." In the same letter he reported a change of plans: an encampment of six hundred lodges of "Pagans" to the west deserved their attention. The letter would be sent on with Captain James Fisk's gold train, one day behind them on the trail.

It was more than appropriate that an army expedition of soldiers and future farmers would cross the Sheyenne a day ahead of a wagon train of gold-seekers as America went looking. Some disparaged this year's Fisk train as composed of "scalawags of all sorts" but for the St. Paul Press it was a "victorious army sent forth by Minnesota to clear the path of emigration and commerce to the Pacific," Fisk and Sibley moving a day apart, two armies sent to clear the path, punish evil, and subdue the earth out from under those who wrongly possessed it.

North of Valley City about twenty miles, I turned west toward the Sheyenne and the General's Second Crossing, which became an early vacation spot, "Sibley's Trail Resort," and then the town of Sibley—where I'd imagined gliding to shore in my canoe after a successful float—with a population of forty. Almost completely dry in the barren summer of 1863, the Sheyenne widened here, the northern bulge of a lake backed up by Valley City's Baldhill Dam. That day I only had a highway map, some photocopied pages from Wright's history, which I hadn't yet read, and the promise of a historic marker nearby. I crossed the Sheyenne, driving over the same and different waters, and pulled up in front of the Sibley Cafe, the only car.

Sitting at the counter, I had the noon special, bratwurst with sauerkraut, a baked potato, and corn, my fork clinking in the silence until another customer came in and settled himself in front of the noon special as well. I asked about Sibley's Crossing, which was *supposed* to be—I'd learned to put things in the historic conditional mood—marked by a boulder. Yeah, the waitress said. Up the road a few miles on the right. "I've always been meaning to go look at that, but I guess I haven't made it yet." She nodded as if her resolve had just been strengthened.

"Isn't *that* it?" the man asked, thumbing toward a raw, six-foot high boulder across the road.

"Mercy no," the waitress said, giving a name I couldn't hear. "He put that up. Found it in his field years ago and brought it down here. Thought it looked nice."

"Hunh," the customer shook his head, turning back to his bratwurst. "I always thought *that* was the marker."

"So you haven't been there?" I asked.

"I'll tell you," she leaned on the counter. "I've lived here eighteen years and I've only gotten as far north as Sharon." I figured that less than twenty-five miles. "Just had to work all the time."

I headed north and found, at an intersection, a cairn of cemented rocks indicating the site of Camp Corning, not the crossing itself—I should have realized how far I was from the river. I drove back through Sibley, considered telling the waitress, decided it didn't matter, and crossed the Sheyenne eastward again.

Turning north, I found a dirt lane—"Public Road," the sign promised—leading back toward the river and I jolted along its tracks to come out onto a high bank. Wright had said "the old rutted trail" could still be seen but I was several decades later and used to such disappearances. Storage bins and farm machinery dotted the broad sides and rim of the silent valley, but clumps of silver sage, a remnant of the prairie, grew at my feet. I tried to feel the original movement of men in the empty afternoon air but I couldn't and I slid back in the car. I hadn't discovered much more than the waitress in her eighteen years.

I used up the rest of the afternoon slowly driving back south paralleling the river, and it was dark by the time I drove into Valley City. At the cafe counter next to me, a man in overalls and plaid shirt, his face blood-caked with deep scratches, was already telling his story to the waitress. He'd hit a deer on a nearby gravel road about fifteen minutes ago, he said, and a little ripple went up my spine. After Sibley crossed the Sheyenne, an elk scared up, some of the men chasing it into the wagon train where it got entangled in the chains of a team. Some similar piece of wilderness had happened just now, and I sat inside a moment, the present echoing a hundred thirty-two years ago. Jeez, he said, shaking his head, still a little shaken but beginning to feel that swaggering sense of luck. He should get that looked at, the waitress said, reaching out toward the side of his head. Yeah, he would, he nodded.

I ate, sorting through notes and discovering my mistake, the actual crossing one township farther south than where I'd stood by the end of a lake trying to imagine men crossing an almost dry river, but it was too late. Yet again, I'd been too easily happy, thinking I found this spot or that while wandering through a series of compromises and I realized it also wasn't possible that

Camp Corning should have coincided so neatly with what would later become a section corner and road intersection. But I'd done enough for one day, and I was tired.

Unlike the general, I could drive 55 miles an hour north to home. The street lights of Aneta—the cafe was closed—glared momentarily bright on the windshield and vanished as I left town. The scattered flares of farmhouses off on the nighttime prairie, and they're farther apart in North Dakota than one might think, reminded me of distant campfires, temporary braveries in a large darkness.

A few weeks later I headed toward Carrington on my last trip with Sibley. Setting up base at Camp Atchison near Binford, he'd taken a smaller contingent westward where the "pagans" were supposedly camped. Camp Kemball of July 22 was southwest of Carrington and I had directions from a local historian, but I failed again. A gravel truck was parked along the road, but the young driver hadn't heard of it. Sorry, he said, he was from Valley City. I drove on into Woodworth, near July 23's Camp Grant, and asked two men working on a roof about any historical marker nearby. Sorry, they were from Carrington. Still, I was among Woodworth's hundred citizens and there was a cafe. As the waitress poured a cup of coffee, I asked her, with no hope, about Sibley's camp.

"Oh, yeah, ask Bill," she said easily, pointing to a table of two boys, a girl, and a middle-aged farmer. "It's on his land."

Bill said hello, agreed, and after coffee I followed his truck several miles before he pulled off the gravel near a large, almost dry marsh. A massive stone bore the bronze marker for Camp Grant, a nearby sign listing the names of three of Sibley's men who had returned, one the father, two the grandfathers, of area farmers. Bill told me about the trouble they'd had getting a rock that heavy into a wagon, dropping it, breaking part of it, the wagon breaking, stories probably more often told than what it commemorated. And who could blame them? Let there be two markers, one for men moving on, another for those who remembered and who came back to stay, the way Longie returned to Lake Tewaukon.

We stood by the fence and looked off to the marsh. A three-mile long lake for Sibley, it was now only a vague oval, auburn grasses at the edge and green in the center. "All those men," Bill said. "Hard to imagine where they'd camp." We stood for a long moment, trying to imagine it.

"See those trees over there?" he finally said. "Must have been a homestead. Around here, any place you see a tree, somebody lived there." He nodded to himself at the observation.

Finally, Bill had to leave and we shook hands. His truck rattled down the gravel road toward the particular trees where *he* lived, and I headed back, not sure if we had been giants filling the prairie air or a pitiful string of little equipments crawling through a vast solitude. I would come close to the Sibley battles tomorrow, I'd planned that, but I wasn't sure what that meant either. I'd just see, I told myself, knowing it was no answer. In Carrington—the first settler had arrived nineteen years after Sibley's expedition—I took a room at the Chieftain Motel, in front of which stood a tall, concrete statue of an Indian in a headdress, staring across the street all night.

The next morning, I drove east toward Binford and reached the marker for Camp Atchison, a small U.S. flag wavering a little in the light breeze. Bill Clandenning recorded the news for July 21: some men from the Fisk train went over to Sibley's camp for dinner, there was thunder and some rain in the evening, and a soldier was accidentally shot. I'd been told that the lake across the road was Sibley Lake and that a grave on the nearby hill was that of the shooting victim that July night.

No one at the house to give permission, I scaled the thick boards of a corral fence and dropped into the pasture. Two horses looked up, then went back to grazing as I crossed the grass and angled up the steep result of glacial shear—ice pressing itself upward over an obstacle and scooping out lakes below as it built higher hills. On top, metal posts carried three strands of barbed wire around a square plot in the ground, the white stone marking George Brent, Company D, 1st Minnesota Mounted Rangers.

Brent may have been drinking—although alcohol was forbidden by Sibley—or, as some reported, he'd gotten news of an inheritance. Whatever the reason, he galloped around the camp in high spirits, firing a pistol, until his horse stumbled on a tent rope and went down, his pistol or the carbine at his saddle discharging.

Inside the plot lay a lichen-covered stone, one more relic pushed down from Canada a millennium ago, and in front of me a dark tuft of cattle hair recently caught on a barb of wire, a gunshot echoing between those two moments of history. There had been ceremonies, but the body had been put in a rough coffin so that it could be removed later. Wright explains it simply: "No one ever took the trouble to go back for it."

A short distance from the hilltop grave and with a view of Sibley Lake, an aluminum lawn chair tilted in the wiry grass. Accepting an invitation not offered, I sat down and stretched out my legs, looking down on the lake—"a handsome sheet of water," Sibley declared—and over the hills, end moraines of stagnant ice.

I relaxed in the sun, the raucous squabbles of geese and ducks lifting up from the lake and the warbles and trills of meadow larks and red-winged blackbirds filling the air around me. To the north was Binford but the first settlement was Blooming Prairie and I liked that better. Scattered down the slope, pasqueflowers sprouted their fuzzy purple petals and I remembered my mother's early memory, lakes of flowers around the rises of prairie grass. A Blooming Prairie.

And a Bloody War. West of where I sat in a lawn chair by a grave, Sibley entered into three decisive engagements. At Big Mound, they came upon a large camp of Sioux, meeting a delegation and one of the peace chiefs, Standing Buffalo, on a nearby hill. Oscar Wall believed the band was about to surrender—they'd known Sibley was coming, had made no effort to move their families or camp, and had requested the meeting. Dr. Weiser had joined the group, shaking hands with Sioux he remembered from his home town in the Minnesota valley when someone—Wall called him an outlaw—fired a revolver and Weiser fell. Surely the killing of Weiser was an individual act, something to be investigated and put into perspective and, just as surely, it would not be. Soldiers sprang to attack and the Sioux to retreat and, failing that, to counterattack.

The accounts of the battle thicken with military language, deployments and flankings, advancing and occupying, lines wheeling to the right and the left, someone gaining and someone "fleeing precipitately." Soon, eighty Sioux were dead and—whether or not Weiser had been scalped—twenty warriors now lay with bloody skulls, evidence of the "white man's barbarity" for West, a practice appalling to Sibley who always forbade it. But what could be said? Col. McPhail told his men it was barbarous but added he wouldn't believe anyone had killed an Indian unless he could see the scalp.

One image from the accounts had stayed with me. Wall had marveled at a "stalwart, muscular Indian" draped in a large U.S. flag who walked out in evident surrender and became the target for a hundred shots. Wounded, he returned fire from his double-barreled shotgun, finally using it as a club before he collapsed. A St. Paul newspaper characterized him as an attacker.

On July 26, after passing a lake where a dead buffalo lay, the soldiers found the remains of the great camp abandoned after the battle at Big Mound, burning large amounts of buffalo and tallow by Sibley's order and gathering up the more valuable buffalo robes left behind only to leave them behind again, too heavy to carry in the Dakota July heat. Attempting to camp later on, they were charged—Wall says "like a hurricane," Marshall says "suddenly as the spring of concealed tigers"—by several hundred Sioux trying to run off the horses and mules that had been picketed. They were rebuffed after a two-hour struggle, and the second encounter was over.

The third battle, Stony Lake on July 28, would be the most memorable. Sibley told West the advancing Sioux were a magnificent sight, "a perfect picture." Smoke tinted the morning air, Wall remembered, "a ruddiness that added spirit to one of the most picturesque military encounters every witnessed." The Sioux, their numbers reinforced from the Missouri lodges thirty miles to the west and probably including Sitting Bull himself, fought—as the phrase has it—with a bravery the soldiers admired. Wall found it "smacking of romance rather than of real endeavor," and descriptions treat it as a tapestry, historic and full-color, two equal masters of their destinies contending in a grand engagement. As it happened, Sibley was on the trail of revenge against warriors he wasn't sure were there and the Sioux were fighting to hold off the soldiers until wives, children, and the elderly could cross the Missouri.

On July 29 Sibley's men arrived at Apple Creek about four miles from present-day Bismarck, and there was some skirmishing, ambushing, "volleys of musketry," but the Sioux were making it across the Missouri and finally, it was done, the battles over, and the army, unable to go any farther from their base camp, turning back.

The Indians had been punished, Wall writes, their loss of property and foods reducing them to "a state of destitution," a kind of victory, although some critics would claim the Sioux were not even demoralized. For West, it had been "the last desperate struggle of the haughty Dakota this side of the Missouri River." On July 31, Sibley read to his troops the general order ending the campaign. "The design of the government in chastising the savages, and thereby preventing, for the future, the raids upon the frontier, has been accomplished." It would be gratifying if "these remorseless savages," Sibley said remorselessly, could have been pursued farther.

On August 1 Wall wrote, "All is joy this morning, for we turn our faces once more toward civilization." The men sang "Home, Sweet Home," strange echoes across the Missouri hills, and returned to Camp Atchison, which passed out of existence eleven days later, a landscape of flattened grounds, small, softening earthworks, the grave-length trenches of cooking fires, and all the trash and treasure ordinary life and extraordinary war leave behind.

In all, 150 Sioux were killed or wounded and 7 soldiers lay dead, enough for several varieties of sorrow. I sat in a lawn chair belonging to the unknown owner of the hill beside an accidental grave overlooking Sibley Lake in late-afternoon shadow, tired of the pushing of currents across the land. I was also tired of the language we used for war, overwhelmed by the number of times

I'd read the nouns "wretches" and "demons" and "savages" with their interchangeable adjectives "naked" and "remorseless." In its origins, *remorse* signifies the past "biting back" at the present and I felt some of that along with *regret*, a word suggesting "to cry out again," to lament anew, words showing the past pushing into the present and the present revisiting the past, and there was enough of both to go around.

Wall rosily claimed the Sibley campaign had taken the lands from the "idle and indolent" and molded them into "the magnificent commonwealth of North Dakota, with its cities and its towns, its schools and its churches, railroads, homes, vast herds and golden fields." A landscape Wall had experienced as "merely a solitude of limitless possibilities" was now "subdued, beautified, glorified."

I sighed noisily and then stood up, a little stiff from sitting that long. I paused at Brent's grave and the timeless piece of Canadian granite and the timeless tuft of cattle hair. I could not imagine what it felt like, one hundred thirty-two years ago, to be on either side of those wars. Yet my grandmother Lottie was born only six years later. My great-grandfathers could have marched with Sibley, doing it for me, without knowing it and without my awareness. I had inherited the regret of both races.

Threading my way around the lake-colored blossoms of pasque, I walked back down, crossed the pasture, scaled the fence, and hunched into my car. Opening the glove compartment, I stowed my military maps, then drove the highway across what was left of the blooming prairie, at home in what two races left behind. Before Sharon and Aneta, I crossed the Sheyenne, which, only a little below me in the gathering night, pretended to know nothing about history.

at the fort, at the village

A week after watching General Sibley depart and heading toward two villages, Fort Ransom and the Cheyenne's single home, I passed the river slicing through the spillways of Bald Hill Dam into concrete-banked channels and on to Valley City. With more than 7,000 people and a state university, it would provide the bustle of "civilization," as travelers on the prairie might call it, and I planned to stay awhile but almost immediately scrapped my plans.

I'd become so accustomed to the silence of open land and mute river that the store windows reflected too brightly, the streets held too many people, the billboards jumbled too many words together.

After the Sheyenne curved placidly around Valley City State University's small campus and beneath an ornate bridge, I found it again under a high trestle. Walking a sandy lane, I brushed through shoulder-high weeds to the bank where a man and woman stood fishing, two glowing red and chartreuse bobbers barely moving in the sluggish current. The young, as everywhere, had painted the trestle's concrete foundations with names or initials and repeatedly their year, new and then quickly old. We were here. We were there.

Who's leaving and staying in Dakota is important to understand, a matter of human geometries. There are the straight lines of property and highway and the ups and downs of income and population, but there is also the circle, as Lowell Goodman had recently shown in *The Economic Health of North Dakota*. Looking at 1936, the year of the state's highest population and number of farms, he found each town served more than a hundred farms in its circle of countryside with an average of 400 acres per farm. The average now at 1,250 acres, the same town drew on only thirty-six farms, the problem more than population decline. As a trade center, Valley City had lost the retail dollars of more than six thousand people and will, by 2010, lose half that again.

It had to do with time and distance. Fargo's sprawl of malls and stores lay to the east and as we had accustomed ourselves to driving half a day into town in the 1900s, we didn't much mind driving over an hour to reach a larger town these days. This pattern, Goodman pointed out, "built by consumer choice," was unchangeable. It was noticed first on Main Street, the movie theater closing, then the furniture store and the grocery, but we couldn't fix it by fixing Main Street. Subsidizing a welding shop or restaurant wouldn't keep young people in the state and we'd waste money trying for businesses such as telemarketing, which, usually paying poorly with few or no benefits, didn't create an employment multiplier.

In *Dakota: A Spiritual Geography,* Kathleen Norris wrote of her own experience in a plains town after the boom years of the 1950s, as a sense of security began to drain away. A development committee was formed but "aspirations scaled down almost immediately," local business interests combining to keep out others, and the committee soon folded. "The sad truth is," Norris wrote as one who'd seen this sad truth closely, "the harder we resist change, and the more we resent anyone who demands change of us, the more we short-change ourselves."

And, Goodman warned, not every community *could* be saved. We should concentrate on the main trade centers—so much for "villages"—that followed the natural economic evolution of the state: Grand Forks, Devils Lake, Minot, and Williston across the top third of the state and Fargo/West Fargo, Wahpeton, Valley City, Jamestown, Mandan/Bismarck, and Dickinson along the bottom. A circle of an hour and half travel time around each of the ten towns included almost every mile of the state.

I leaned against the girders of the trestle in the gentle sun, almost nostalgic for the unimaginably recent high school graduation years, the fishermen's bright plastic bobbers still barely moving on the Sheyenne's brown surface. Then I climbed into the car, backed through a thick drift of glacial sand to the street, and left Valley City to its future.

I drove straight south, the river crossing under me a couple of times, and came upon "Kathryn," the daughter of the Northern Pacific president in 1900, spelled out across a hill in white stones, the Y and the N almost hidden by grass. The Sheyenne turned along the main street—Kathryn had a population of 289 in 1920, 72 now—and I did too, past empty false-front stores and the old cafe with a huge Pepsi sign, its red and white fading to rust and fog. The bridge was out at the end of town, so I retraced a mile, turned east, and joined the river again.

Soon I was driving Highway 46 through the fields of wheat and corn with occasional acres of sunflowers. A few years ago I'd stopped at the Standing Rock a couple of miles east—the highest point in the county, sacred to the Sioux and remarked upon by both Nicollet and Sibley—so I passed, not knowing I'd return that night, and rattled toward Fort Ransom. Some came here on their way to somewhere else, the first German Russian Mennonites, even the small colony of gypsies who bought a few farms nearby with gold coins and drifted away again. But many traveled to be exactly here, the Sheyenne becoming in one generation "a Norwegian river" for two hundred miles upstream into Wells County.

And here, around a curve, was one of them, a homemade sign announcing "The Historic Slattum Cabin." A pair of overalls on the clothesline and a few red geraniums on each side of the open door invited a traveler, so I ducked in and read the typed sheets of family history tacked to the logs, sunlight slanting in through the window.

Selling their farm in Slattum, Norway, in 1869, Theodore and Jorgena left for Minnesota with their five children, a sixth being born on the trip. Theodore worked—a seventh born—until Dakota opened up in 1879 whereupon he walked to the Sheyenne Valley with $40 in his pocket, claimed the homestead I was standing on, brought back his family—an eighth born but dying on the way—and settled to stay. Their ninth, Ole, was the first white child born in the township.

Theodore lived out his life in 1902 and Jorgena in 1914, the children and grandchildren accounted for in their various new homes as well as a grandson, Carroll, still on the original homestead. Emerging from the cabin, old clothes stirring on the line and new flowers blooming, I felt the Slattums had just stepped out themselves. Down the road, I passed Carroll's mailbox, "Slattum" in white block letters on a prosperous-looking red barn.

A few miles later, I came to Fort Ransom. The old fort had been up on the hill from 1867–1872, but the town, founded in 1880, nestled in trees at the bottom. Passing a dozen of the one hundred and five people a sign had declared, I drove slowly past Del's Upholstery, Antiques, the JS Corral, and the newly-constructed cabins of the Viking View Resort below a small hill on which stood the tall statue of a Norwegian warrior, horned helmet and all, looking out over the settlement.

I drove on into the state park, set up camp, and cooked a quick meal, ending with a cup of coffee I sipped as I walked through the brush behind me to find the Sheyenne. Poet Thomas McGrath's grandparents had lived near here, his grandmother seeing an Indian, "the last one perhaps," ascending the Sheyenne in a canoe and I dutifully looked upstream, the brownish-silver water winding through fallen branches from each bank. As a boy, his father had seen them camped each spring and fall where he herded cattle, but those were old stories. "The road outside the window was 'our' road," McGrath wrote and then it became "the road on which everyone went away." I went away myself, driving back into town.

At the crowded JS Corral, people were at home. I edged between two tables—four men drinking beer and playing pinochle and five middle-aged women talking and sipping from tall frosted glasses—to stand at the bar, order a scotch from the barmaid, and look around. At the far end, a boy and a long-haired Indian girl played pool. At the chorus of the jukebox song, he bawled along "Keep on—keep on *ridin'*!" "Star Trek: The Next Generation" glowed from the muted TV high in a corner, Commander Riker being captured by a blonde lionish alien. Nobody was watching.

Shirley—maybe the S of the JS Corral—sat at a nearby table with an older couple, the man with a hearing aid. "Fourth of July," the woman was saying to Shirley, "and I sat on the grass to watch and I got chigger bites! All over me!"

"Oh, I heard that," Shirley laughed.

To my right, all the pinochle players stood up. "Damn, that's enough for me," one said loudly coming around the bar to join the barmaid, probably the J of the Corral's name, let's even say "Jay."

"I don't usually like spinach salad," Shirley said to the woman, "but she had this hot dressing and it was good."

"Keep on *ridin'*!" bawled the boy at the pool table.

A girl came out, serving the couple with Shirley. "I knew you were here—" the girl said to the husband and he turned his other ear toward her. "I knew you were here when I saw that order in the kitchen." I treated myself to another scotch, then another.

"Let's play golf tomorrow," Jay suggested to a customer.

"Nah, I can't. I gotta do some construction up north."

"Up Nort?" Jay asked with a grin, others along the bar taking turns at a Norwegian accent. "Up Nord?" "Oop Nor?"

"Up by Kathryn," the construction worker answered.

Just before the barmaid, without looking up, changed the channel to a baseball game, Riker had found himself among more aliens—a Romulon, a Klingon—and I felt a little alien myself although we were all here in the village, Norwegians and non-Norwegians, Indians, maybe cowboys, all of us guarded by an artificial Viking on the hill outside.

I paid and slid a little unsteadily off the stool. "Have a nice trip," the barmaid said, knowing I was on one, and I thanked her. Back at my camp, woozy from the scotch and dazzled by the number of stars in the unpolluted darkness, I rolled my sleeping bag out beside the tent and lay staring up, the Sheyenne behind me riffling a little whisper, my head to the west so that, a Cheyenne map laid out toward the east, I was aligned with that world. Well, more or less. Their true east is the sunrise during the Sun Dance in early June, a semi-cardinal direction although to them I'd be the one living a little off angle. I used the North Star to change direction just a little, but how could I know what something as simple as a different compass felt like, much less understand anything deeper?

I'd thought of the Cheyenne as archetypal warriors and buffalo hunters, but to them it was a new way of life. We worried about our familiar hometowns fading as economics changed, but in two centuries their landscape shifted a thousand miles, their farmers turning into nomadic hunters in little more than a generation. It was dreamlike, I was almost dreaming it myself, this one people who divided themselves into southern and northern, who gave up one life for another and then another, a river coming together and flowing apart, and I fell deeper asleep.

Here was the story. The Tsis-tsis-tsas, the *People*, lived in a huge cave until a light appeared to lead them up onto the earth where they traveled to a large river and stayed and then moved on, arriving at the shore of a large lake where they found abandoned tools and stayed a long time and then moved westward, reaching a flat country and living by a river until they were attacked and then moved on, arriving at the Missouri. "Stately Indians," the Lewis and Clark journals say, "rich in horses and dogs," who "formerly lived in a Village and Cultivated Corn on the Cheyene [*sic*] River."

They had probably lived in villages of related families between the Great Lakes and Hudson Bay before they left and came to the great marshes of southern Ontario and northern Minnesota. About 1675, they moved farther south to the mouth of the Minnesota River where they began planting corn and building earth lodges, but moved on after about twenty-five years under pressure from the Cree and Assiniboine who were armed with rifles from British and French traders. Pushed and pressed, the Tsis-tsis-tsas began building fortification ditches and log stockades.

The migration continued, one village settling, another passing it and stopping to settle, a series of loops so that some lived in Minnesota, some on the Sheyenne, some on the Missouri at the same time yet in different stages of cultural movement, a people continually adjusting to change. Acquiring horses about 1750, the men hunted while the women, children, and elderly stayed in the village, tanning hides and tending crops. When they arrived at the Missouri, they could trade for vegetables from the Mandan and Arikara so they developed their hunting skills even more.

It was also probably near the Missouri—some say north of there, some the pipestone quarries of Minnesota—that the Tsis-tsis-tsas met themselves in the form of the Suhtai, the two groups lining up to fight and realizing they were speaking the same language, perhaps separated as they left their first watery country. This joining formed the dual ancestry of the modern nation with its two medicine items, the Sacred Buffalo Hat of the Suhtai and the Sacred Arrows of the Tsis-tsis-tsas given to them by Sweet Medicine, their first law-giver.

There would be more history after the Missouri, but for now I only dreamed of where they had come from to settle their village on the Sheyenne. Classically, says John Moore, they were a "stable, integrated, homogeneous society, remarkable for the chastity of the women and the ruling authority of the Council of Forty-Four" and had a cultural preference for formality and order, even though a band on the Republican River in 1860 wouldn't reflect the same culture as one on the Missouri in 1805. They moved through history "in a series of national identities," the old village one stopping place on that journey, and I slept with my body almost toward the east.

Waking in the bright sun, already too warm, I pumped up the camp stove and fixed breakfast. I'd tried to keep my plan—sleeping in a two-hundred-year-old village—in the back of my mind although I'd badgered an anthropologist for the legal description of the site. There was something important about an all-night stay, inviting a kind of meditation on the past, but also something questionable, romantic in the worst sense, and surely illegal to borrow a neighbor's pasture. Still, I had a lot of time before nightfall.

Above the village of Fort Ransom, I ambled around the emptiness of the fort itself, a flagless pole in a grassy field, small depressions labeled "Captain's Quarters," "Commissary." Not particularly large, two hundred men, it lasted not particularly long, five years, guarding the trail from the Red to the Missouri, made obsolete when the Northern Pacific reached Jamestown and Fort Seward was built, lasting six years and ending up, I knew from another trip, another bare patch of grass with an empty flagpole on a bluff overlooking a town.

Then I started off, surrendering myself to a day of circling my destination, visiting village after village. Driving north I came into Enderlin, busy enough that day with its one thousand citizens, the business district torn up into dirt streets, new sidewalks and curbs here, yawning craters there. I stopped at the Friend Tavern for lunch, more and more customers crowding in, farmers, wives, young males ready for their shift at the huge sunflower plant I passed as I left town. Grain trucks ramrodded down gravel roads, swirling up long clouds behind them, the backs of the sunflowers gray and shaggy with dust.

It was a drowsy afternoon in Sheldon—358 people in 1910, half that now, not a growth point, but still here—and I bought an apple at Mel's Country Grocery and watched a railroad car being filled with wheat at the elevator. The Northern Pacific arrived in 1882, the town incorporating two years later and becoming a center for amateur baseball, winning the state title in 1895, a century after the Cheyenne left their village—a long time, and not a long time.

A few miles south I walked through Anselm's Lutheran Cemetery—Kelm, Froemke, Schmidtke, and Hanelt—to where the hillside slanted down a half-mile of sunflowers to the Sheyenne, and, a little farther south, through the Evangelical Cemetery—Nohr, Kemmer, and Christmann. After that, I turned randomly off and onto a series of county roads until I misplaced myself, surprised when I came to Wyndmere—five hundred people for the last three decades, the Tastee Freeze for sale—and I stopped to look at the map. About twenty miles north of Sibley's camp on Lake Tewaukon, I was twenty miles south of the ancient village and it was time to find it. West of Wyndmere, combines moved through the half-harvested wheat like army tanks, gun-barrels spouting grain, all this dimly seen through the hazy dust of chaff, turned to a spattering golden red by the 5 P.M. sun. I turned off Highway 27 onto a gravel road.

The Cheyenne village was settled at least by 1724 and probably abandoned around 1790 after a Chippewa attack, perhaps revenge, perhaps jealousy for favoring the Sioux. After the village was destroyed, some traveled on to the Missouri, maybe some to the Black Hills or Nebraska or south to join the Arapaho, the People traveling over the waters of a national identity.

In the early years, most had good opinions of the Cheyenne, "the genuine children of nature," reported an officer on the 1825 Atkinson expedition. "They live in constant exercise of moral and Christian virtues, though they know it not." The artist George Catlin thought there was "no finer race of men than these in North America." Still, there was war and the rumors of war. The establishment of Bent's Fort began the fur-trading period, which began the liquor period, washing over the Cheyenne with disastrous results as the currents of war continued to rise and turn.

The Minnesota Uprising and Sibley's and Sully's marches stirred things up but the Cheyenne had been relatively peaceful. Chiefs, including Black Kettle, had sent letters proposing peace and were brought to Denver for discussion in the summer of 1864 but orders from on high suggested they hadn't suffered enough. The *Rocky Mountain News* asserted that quiet could be obtained only by "a few months of active extermination against the red devils."

Extermination hit its high, or low, point at Sand Creek. Less than twenty years before Wyndmere was established, Left Hand's Arapaho had been sent to camp on the Colorado creek on their own reservation, Black Kettle's Cheyenne joining them in a village of six or seven hundred. Col. John Chivington, a militia commander and a Methodist minister—God still watchful over his command to subdue the earth—set out with his force to find the warrior Dog Soldiers, or avoid them, and rode to the peace camp at Sand Creek, a U.S. flag fluttering from one of the tipis. Chivington attacked at dawn. "Nits make lice," the minister reportedly said, leading his men to gun down, mutilate, and dismember children, women, and old men in a notorious massacre, convincing the tribes that extermination was the official U.S. policy. They fought back with their allies, closing down the Platte River Road, burning farms and ranches, pushing the frontier eastward by several hundred miles.

But the *wasichu* military could not be resisted forever and soon the Northern Cheyenne were moved to Oklahoma to join the Southern in a common landscape of homesickness, disease, and hunger. These were the years, as Mari Sandoz describes in *Cheyenne Autumn*, of graft and theft on the reservations—sugar mixed with sand, clothing that fell apart in water—and of army contractors making millions while malaria, dysentery, and simple starvation threatened the Cheyenne's very existence in 1877 and again in 1878. A group finally broke out of Oklahoma, most captured and held at Nebraska's Ft. Robinson until they broke out again, most killed as they tried to move north and home. After all this, the Northern Cheyenne were "allowed" back into Montana, finally in their land except for those who had starved or died of sickness, or had been shot or bayoneted or frozen. Except for those.

I turned along the Sheyenne hidden by woods and thickets and in a mile or so came to a field road leading to a low bluff. Parking by the gate, I wrote a note saying I was just visiting the site, tucked it under my windshield wiper, and shouldered my sleeping bag. I followed the dusty cut of a cattle trail up to a bare, pockmarked pasture, the grassy sinks of more than sixty earthlodges. Its absent citizens had followed, Moore says, "a very common and successful economic strategy," intensively tending vegetable gardens and scheduling buffalo hunts onto the plains. The village had been, like Valley City, a growth point on the prairie, lives spreading out from that home and circling back in again.

It was almost nine, the sky a swirl of pink and apricot clouds, and I walked among the hollows, finally choosing one near the edge of the bluff, throwing my sleeping bag into it, and lying down. I hadn't noticed any mosquitoes before, but they came now, and I swept my hat around my head. In the middle of the "ancient capital" of the Cheyenne, as Wright put it, stood a rusted Chevy pickup. From the distance came the roar of a grain truck laboring down a road.

I had some thoughts about the Slattum cabin, a center of dispersal that still existed, and even of the original Vikings, the need for new lands sending them off over the waters, and the inhabitants of Fort Ransom, some leaving, some staying. I thought of my own childhood home, a little geography I'd memorized, the slant of the driveway up to the road, the weedy ditch to the rear, the stucco house torn down when my parents finally moved, and thought of the children who'd memorized the body of their first village, no doubt the last village of the very old, the center of a world for seventy years.

Cramped in my pit, gritty and dusty from the day's drive and still swatting mosquitoes, I uncurled and walked to the edge of the bluff. Col. Marshall, visiting with other Sibley officers that July 4, found a spring at the bottom but it had disappeared, even the Sheyenne leaving, the hollow below me an old ox-bow, the foot of the bluff eroded, muffled with grass. I walked back to my hole and sat on the edge.

The Cheyenne, Sandoz said, perceived life as a "continuous and all-encompassing" flow in which things—man, tree, rock, cloud—exist "simultaneously in all the places they had ever been; and all things that had ever been in a place were always in the present there, in the being and occurring." And here I was, ice withdrawing and river retreating yet still here in bluff and bend, the Cheyenne gone, rings of openings into the earth, the Cheyenne here always, and I sat inside echo after echo in the first of the gathering darkness.

I turned—a spell broken—at the sudden rumble of a pickup lurching down the lane to stop beside my car for several minutes, the driver not getting out, before rumbling on. I had a flash of concern, not knowing how strongly he felt about his ownership, but how much did I really want to stay the night anyway? Jarred out of a mood, I sat in only a field of dusty rough grass and sunken slumps, more mosquitoes arriving by the minute. I wanted to leave the village to itself. I shouldered my bag and walked back down to the car, looking back up at the bluff for a long moment, needing somewhere to sleep, then making my decision. There was another place with suitable mystery.

Miles later and long after dark, I turned off the highway north of Fort Ransom, bumped a mile or so slightly upward, parked in the gravel lot and climbed the rest of the hill to the Standing Rock. That it was both sacred and a landmark made it the center of something for tonight. The rock itself, now only a dark shape against the sky, was a cone-shaped chunk of granite about four feet tall set upright on a raised mound of earth.

Although the air had been still as I drove, a strangely fresh breeze blew over the hill and I slid into my sleeping bag. Nicollet, camping here, had seen twenty-seven herds of buffalo and listened to their passing throughout the night, and I could hear a combine still churning in the distance. Single farmyards sparkled small fires, a haze of light glowed over Lisbon, and the three red lights of a tower flashed to the southwest. I slept, half-slept, exhausted but on edge, sinking away and coming back up again into the chill night air.

Earlier I'd had the chance to talk to Eugene, friend of a friend, a Cheyenne leader who was periodically living in Grand Forks. I sat on the couch while he took the chair against the balcony window, his head silhouetted against the glare of afternoon light, his face sometimes half-lit, sometimes in darkness. I asked a question I don't remember about the village on the river that he answered briefly and then he began, in that soft hushing of syllables like nothing so much as wind in the grass: "Let me tell you about myself."

One night, friends and neighbors assembled in his front yard, asking him to lead one of the five Cheyenne societies, as his grandfather and father had done, and he'd said yes. He went to Oklahoma to learn what to say and do, what not to say and do, ceremonially and in life. For four years he went to the Sun Dance, two days and nights of dancing without food or water—"I'm glad that's over," he grinned. The third year he saw his totem animal, and he motioned to a picture I couldn't clearly see. As the leader of his society he had a right-hand man and a left-hand man, each with another at his side, who lived on the reservation and phoned him when they needed to.

His young son—I'd met the quick-eyed boy before with his mother—needed to know both worlds, he told me, the old and the new. For example, as a child he used to play with pieces of bone so look at this. He brought out a plate of bones he'd cut into slices, polished and varnished, showing me how a child could stack them, the shining pieces clicking in his hands. Then he brought out sections of backbone. "See, this would be a horse," he said, cantering a gray vertebrae across the back of his hand. The smaller ones were colts. "Oh, here," he said, picking up a gray, weathered bone and moving it slowly. "Here's a real old horse." His eyes sparkled at his joke, his lips tracing only a slight curve upward.

"We're taught to respect everything," he said. "Even rocks." He produced a smooth oval stone. If you worked all day and were tired and sore you could heat this stone on the stove and then wrap it in rawhide and put it on you—he placed it a little behind his shoulder—and then also pray and in fifteen or twenty minutes you'd feel all right again. "So even rocks are good," he said, setting it on the coffee table.

He kept saying "respect" and at first it seemed the kind of word whites pretended Indians used—on the order of "respect for Mother Earth," which we often mouth with little sense of either deep respect or that large a mother—but it was his constant theme. And respect for people as well. You needed tact. If there was a problem, if someone was angry, you found a way to gracefully withdraw because maybe the next day they'd realize they said something angrily or something bad. Be tactful. And be honest. And respect everything.

There were lots of problems on the reservation, he said sadly, but they were trying to deal with them. Sometimes he'd be called about someone who needed disciplining and he'd leave for Montana the next day. Or else he'd say, "Let the Crazy Dogs take care of it," and they would reprimand the person and if that didn't work— I missed the next low phrase but understood it as an ostracism.

It had been hard last winter, he said. Last fall, the Sacred Hat, one of Sweet Medicine's two gifts, was taken from its keeper.

There'd been deaths among the people, two a week they said, bad medicine in the air. That spring they'd had sweats, ceremonies, lectures. That summer, a blessing had been held at Bear Butte and a runner took the eagle staff the two hundred miles to Lame Deer, Montana.

If I wanted to know other things, he said, standing up, he had some videotapes I could watch and then ask about, but I said I'd just talk to him again. The next time I called, he was gone, and when he was back in town I was gone, and the next I heard he was back in Montana. I felt I'd learned very little and also that I couldn't have learned more at that point. I knew I'd remember the importance of respect, respect, and the importance of the stone on the coffee table and the stack of bones and the little animals of vertebrae on the window sill behind him in the gray glare of the light, his words hushing against themselves, the breath of a people losing and finding themselves over and over.

I woke about 5:30, a mosquito buzzing in my ear, and sat up beside the Standing Rock, its beveled tip pointing to Venus. I pulled my sleeping bag around my shoulders and sat on that vantage point to watch, in the gradually lightening sky, the world come back again.

Sweet Medicine had prophesied the white man's arrival and Fred Last Bull, the Keeper of the Sacred Arrows in the late fifties, remembered his warning, that the white man's food would be sweet and the Cheyenne would forget their own. It was all coming true, Last Bull said. "We eat it and we forget." Ten years later, John Stands In Timber said Sweet Medicine had warned the Cheyenne their ways would change, that they'd become worse than crazy. "I am sorry to say these things," Sweet Medicine said, "but I have seen them, and you will find that they come true."

By six, a couple of crows started calling from the wooded bottomland. One cow bawled from the southeast and, a few seconds later, another from the southwest. More crows had something to say as the stratus clouds in the east went red to orange to gray, then darkened against the day's light, and more cattle bawled. I shrugged off my sleeping bag and walked the few feet to Standing Rock, touching it like a pilgrim. The coolness of the granite was almost a shock.

One of Stands In Timber's favorite songs contained the line, "My friends, only the stones stay on earth forever," and it seemed this one would. It would also remain an emblem of wandering, a dark rock ribboned with icy diagonals of feldspar and quartz, a map of the flow and push of creation itself, an obelisk rammed hundreds of miles by ice to stand above the rolling sediment of the plains. In the middle of a prairie space, the standing rock stood, like the deserted village, in the middle of time as well, all things simultaneously in all the places they had ever been.

past and future in the grasslands

It was a warm August morning when I stopped at the cafe in Leonard before my foray into the Sheyenne National Grasslands. Two men and a woman bent over coffee at the table near the kitchen and when I sat down by the front window the woman got up smiling—"What'cha need this morning?"—poured me a cup and returned to her table.

The talk was solemn, an accident that weekend, an elderly couple hit by a gravel truck as they came from a side road onto the highway. Didn't they need a yellow light at that intersection? the woman wondered. Or at least some roughing on that side road, a man said. They discussed who was driving the truck and who he worked for, and then turned to past accidents. One of the men got up, set his cup and saucer in a plastic tub by the counter and held the door open for another man to enter and sit down in the same chair, making it three again.

I was among neighbors, and it was easy to think of past neighbors, the settlers of Sheyenne Township a few miles south whom I'd met in the informal history Mrs. Haugen had written. There was Andrew Berg who'd built the first log cabin in the area, telling the next generation about the seven tipis on a nearby ridge: he'd never bothered them and they'd never bothered him. And the Knutsons, Thyge buying a Laval cream-separator and becoming "The Cream King of Sandoun," which was now McLeod, the early residents tired of being called after the area's sandy dunes. One of Anne Knutson's winter memories would always stay with me: no trees for protection, their house and barn could drift over with snow so they took the shovel into the house at night to dig themselves out in the morning. I'd wondered what kind of sleep that might prompt.

Mrs. Haugen's history included other locals—"Fisher" Olson, named for his favorite activity, or "Pegleg" Nelson who took his leg off in fights to use as a weapon or heave at wayward cattle—but there was another note, the memorial tone of how we leave our names on the land. Christopher "Columbus" Larson lived in a shack up on what was called Columbus Hill, Page Hill was where the Pages lived and a great sledding place too, and the only remnant of the pioneer home of Pauline Johnson was a vacant hole folks called the Pauline Cellar for years.

Everyone in Sheyenne Township knew about the Martin Ranch, located on Iron Springs in the sand dunes along the river, begun in 1900 with more than 3,000 acres. Ted Martin was interested in the past, collecting Indian artifacts, and in the future, helping start the Farmers Union and the Farmer's Holiday Association, although the ranch succumbed to the present of 1928, sold for taxes because Sheyenne Township reflected the fortunes of the state.

Although the cover of a 1920 North Dakota immigration pamphlet featured Demeter, the Greek Goddess of Harvest, holding a shield offering eight promises—beginning with "Better Grain Grades" and ending with "Opportunity and Prosperity for All"—it was the beginning of Depression and Dustbowl and Drought. A year later, the War Finance Corporation began liquidating farm loans, the larger central banks sucking the reserves out of small-town banks, and it got worse. Prices dropped, livestock prices hit an all-time low, farms slid into failure by the hundreds, clouds of dust overwhelmed the countryside, and the worst droughts came since settlement. From 1935 to 1940, eighty-six thousand people left the state.

Sheyenne Township was a small part of those problems because only about forty-four families depended on the grasslands but the same currents moved through and over them. Some lost mortgages, some left to work elsewhere, and the government bought up land now proven sub-marginal for farming and then allowed grazing rights for cattle. By 1934, a third of the taxes were delinquent and half the forty-four Sheyenne Township families were on relief. Three years later, the year I was born, the government took over Andrew Berg's land and tore down Sheyenne Township's first cabin.

The area was now a federal property, small enough—70,000 acres compared to more than a million in the Little Missouri Grasslands in the west—but still representing the larger problems of grass and politics. That summer Sen. Domenici introduced the Livestock Grazing Act, designed to take regulation of grasslands away from the Forest Service, and North Dakota's Sen. Dorgan wrote an amendment, helped by a Mr. Winter, President of the Association of National Grasslands. The issue I heard was multiple use: everyone who pumped oil or watched birds or ran cattle or hiked on public land would have an equal say. A Forest Service friend of mine called the bill "a real right-wing dandy" pushed by western ranchers. Grazing had always been the dominant use—he grazed a few head himself—but the bill would give almost total control of national land to the ranchers. The state's game and fish director predicted less wildlife, particularly ground-nesting birds, and Mr. Winter used the landowners-are-the-best-stewards argument, which has turned out to be true sometimes and false at other times but always rings well, especially in the ears of the stewards. The bill languished and disappeared. It was still waiting, I was sure, to come back up again.

By now there were eight or so men in the cafe, drinking coffee and talking about the weekend's accident. There are about three hundred people in Leonard—five hundred in 1930—but nobody else came in. I took a sip of coffee, the sun almost too hot through the window. I could see railroad tracks to the south, and the trimmed lawns of the few houses, everything in its human place, but beyond that and beyond the wheat fields ran an older flow, centuries of land and water and grass. I took a last sip of coffee, paid my bill in change, and stepped out, blinking in the bright sunlight of Leonard's empty main street.

I'd been through the town, and the gigantic delta of an ancient river spreading into Lake Agassiz a month or so ago. A friend found me studying the Sheyenne and said I should meet her Uncle

Lester from Leonard so one afternoon Lester and I drove the back roads in his pickup, coming again and again to the river.

Lester was some of the local grassland history himself. His parents had farmed here and his generation started the grazing business, Lester a past president of the Stockmen's Association. Pure Norwegian, he told me as he drove, and his wife, Leila, was Swedish. He was excited their grandchildren added mixtures of Irish and Spanish. Even a bit of Indian, he said, releasing the wheel for a second to hold his hands a few inches apart, and then taking a turn off the county road.

We drove into the wooded bottomlands on his property and took a walk. Lester knew a lot about grazing and, recently named North Dakota Tree Farmer of the Year, about trees. You judge timber by gauging the distance before the first branch, he pointed out, helping me practice this skill as we walked through the woods. That was elm. This was basswood. White oak over there. This was nice in the fall, he said. Last September, some senior citizens had taken a bus trip to Minnesota for "the colors." They didn't realize how colorful it could be here. They'd seen it so much, he guessed, it didn't look new. That was an ironwood over there. We turned and headed back toward the car.

Early settlers had cut wood along the river, and I asked if it could still be logged. Well, it'd be hard now. A neighbor had wanted to pay him per tree and haul them out with a Cat but that would batter the underbrush too much and kill young trees, so he'd said no. Here was white oak again. He loved white oak, he said, running his fingers over the bark and looking up to see how high the first branch was.

When we came over a rise I turned one way and he nodded the other. People had gotten lost around here and out on the grasslands too. Oh, yeah. He'd brought down some deer hunters once.

Clouds covered up the sun and they got completely turned around. A high school student got lost for a whole day. Another time a Boy Scout.

We drove on through pleasant fields and more tensions. It had been a wet summer and Lester pointed to puddles in the fields. He knew a farmer who'd just applied for an irrigation permit, his fields already partially flooded and I'd heard something about that. Fargo was expanding its need for water—a corn processing plant in the works—and some farmers, this was the story, were buying up permits they didn't need to protect their interests against the city's.

He drove me to the Runck Chateau, a rural restaurant on the old Power farm he'd known first as a country store. He'd speared fish in the Sheyenne and ridden a horse all over and I got a fleeting sense of boyhood days spent riding throughout this world of grass and woodlands, the sky stretching above, that kind of eternity. But here's what he wanted to show me, he said, behind the restaurant, the largest cottonwood in North Dakota—well, what was left of the it. A sign posted the gigantic stump's dimensions and I wrote them down in a notebook page I never found again.

Back in his truck, we toured the crops along the edges of the timber. You had to know the land, he said, both in the past and future, what *had* been done—he pointed to a field that always grew good hay but this year the owner put in corn and failed— and what *might* be tried. Over there, one farmer was going to plant garlic and that was a first and maybe a good idea. Then we pulled around a corner to find a huge half-harvested field of carrots.

Three trucks sat bogged in ruts at the edge of the field, a huge carrot-picker stranded in the middle of a row. Lester admired machinery in general and had never seen one of these before, so we slogged our way out to it. Along the rows lay the battered casualties of harvest and at the south end a huge pile of mangled waste rose, bright orange chunks against the black earth. As we started back, he selected half a dozen carrots, the largest I'd ever seen, from the muddy ridge of a row. "Take some home," he suggested, and I became his accomplice.

The next stop was a bridge over the Sheyenne to show me North Dakota's biggest white oak. "Right over there," he pointed into the woods and I saw it, or said I did. Beside the bridge sprawled a pile of logs, fifteen or twenty feet high, hauled out from around the pilings to relieve the pressure. The shallow river was at least twenty feet below us but it could, Lester said, flood right up to the bridge, maybe over. He had something else to show me so we drove, the road curving to follow the river, until we were forced to take the loop of a newly graded road, the old road eaten away as the cutbank sharpened. We sat and looked beyond that to the grim cut of the next swath, whiskered with tree roots and grasses. Had to move the road, he said with a mixture of resignation and respect, and probably have to move it again.

On the way home, we made one more stop, a snowy white Lutheran church. "Want you to see this," Lester said. In the entry way, illuminated by appropriately holy shafts of sunlight, stood a table he'd made out of his own white oak and donated to the church. His fingers passed lightly over the gleaming wood and I said it was beautiful. He kept looking down, his hand moving as if he were assembling it again, smoothing it, finishing. He nodded in satisfaction—what work means to the world and what wood means—and we left, closing the shining door behind us.

Leila asked if I'd stay to dinner and I said yes to ham, potatoes, peas, and a green salad around the small table in the kitchen with oddly familiar china. I felt like a child at grandmother's house, although I was closer to an old bachelor invited for dinner. Afterward, I drove home north through the valley while six mud-streaked carrots of prodigious size rolled back and forth on the floor of the backseat.

Today, south of Leonard, I gently slid through the hills on the eastern side of the grasslands, a brochure beside me, until I came to a parking area, the trailhead for this section of the grandly named North Country National Scenic Trail. When finished, it would go three thousand miles, from the Adirondacks of New York across Ohio and southern Michigan, climb up to Lake Superior, then through Minnesota to North Dakota. Ultimately, it would follow the Sheyenne Valley north and northwest, reversing the way I'd come, past forts and encampments, Lutheran cemeteries and log-jams and reservations, to end in Lake Sakakawea.

Only planning to walk in a few miles, certainly not as far as the Sheyenne, I set off with a small plastic water bottle hooked to my belt, across a pasture, through a gate, and entered into Nature again or at least out of sight of my old world. The trail was marked by blue-on-white triangles on posts 500 feet apart, so a hiker could follow a general direction without a trail, but there'd been more trail-riders than walkers, the horses cutting a sandy gash so deep I started to stagger from side to side. I moved out onto the land, ranging one way and another, guessing where the markers might go and cutting off through a cluster of oaks on a small rise to find the next one or the one after that. After a while, a little tired and quite warm, I stopped to rest inside the flickering shade of an oak, finding a small place of prospect to look out across a miniature valley.

According to the brochure, this was oak savanna, a purely American word—*zabana* in the original Taino, those people who'd sent a shower of arrows to welcome Columbus—and it was also veldt, from the Dutch and, earlier from our Indo-European ancestors, *pele*, the root of field and flat, of level and plain and the palm of our hand. In Greek, the verb *planasthai* signified wandering from the idea of "spreading out" the way the land did, and I was wandering into older and older times myself. I thought of the open savannas we humans had come from and found myself crouching as if I were watching for prehistoric game although I didn't know what ancestor I was pretending to be.

Human evolution had seemed to me young, a grand parade of progress, but we had learned more: it was less a continuous stream than a series of loops and stops and starts again, "odd shifts," Stephen Jay Gould calls it, "and backings and forthings." Some species like us, some not, wandered the veldts of our beginnings. I peered out. Across the valley, a grove of bur oak went all silver as a breeze turned up the whitish undersides of its leaves, but no game ventured into the small hollow so, taking a drink of tepid water, I came out of hiding into the bright sun.

I moved off to parallel the trail but when I turned back toward it a few minutes later, there were no trail-markers in sight. Thinking of Lester's warning about getting disoriented in the grasslands, I moved on, knowing my confusion wouldn't last— I'd hit the river if I walked straight west—and enjoying that delicious feeling of being lost only momentarily and when it doesn't matter.

It also helped me realize I was alone, a familiar feeling that summer, but standing beside a cabin or in a cemetery or driving an empty gravel road was different. Here, the trail out of sight, nothing indicated the slightest human presence. Thoreau wrote that legally owning a property was less worthy than owning it with one's eyes but this piece of earth couldn't be possessed that way either. Although landscape is larger than we are and we can't own the mountain vista, we can identify a peak by its shape.

But grassland has another nature, both here and not quite here. The land lifted and fell in the rhythms of sand and wind and water, smoothly regular and intricately varied, a cluster of oak trees lifting up here and then there, islands that the grassland washed around. I moved and felt I wasn't moving. Not the endlessness of open prairie, this was another kind of infinity, equally hard to portray. A quarter-mile ahead lay the horizon of a hill or the border of a grove of trees that gave way to the next dip and rise and horizon. I walked at the center of a small world, the way we animals live, carrying our little finite circles of attention with us, hunting or gathering or migrating through.

Hotter now—the sun was fierce but heat also welled up from the earth—and a little tired, I felt flooded with the sheer variety surrounding me. The slight breeze wavered the fuzzy foreground this way and that into a heady blur. An oval of sumac seemed to surge up along a hillside. A splash of sage trickled down a small ravine. The grass itself was yellow and green and white in the sunshine, or brown, blue-green, ochre, dull crimson, individual threads unraveling from a pattern and being woven together again.

Dizzy in the indefinite softness surrounding me, I felt something at work overwhelming the present. Grasses came from seeds and I was surrounded by trillions of them, tons of sun-bursting potential. I was surrounded by Seed itself, the root that gives us "sow" and "season," and I had gone back that far. I was in the center of pure Season, a wave of nature swelling into the future unmindful of itself, certainly unmindful of me as I walked on into the middle of a billowing, and yet almost motionless, blossom of warm energy.

When I came to a stock tank and windmill, I rejoined the trail and rested. The windmill, half machine and half natural law, helped bring me back into the practical present, from the wooded grasslands where buffalo had grazed to where cattle were now and where buffalo might be again, where we held onto the land at the same time it slipped through our fingers. In Dakota we often felt inside of everything and, simultaneously, like outsiders. This feeling had a long history and it apparently would have a long future.

About three months after my windmill visit, *The New York Times* asked "Is North Dakota necessary?" in an article that characterized our region as "populated increasingly by lonely old women and sustained by farm programs, Social Security, and Medicare." This wasn't new—Thomas McGrath had earlier observed "the she-towns of the farmlands," the "widow sodalities"—but it set the stage for a familiar play. Senator Dorgan sniffed impatiently at "eastern magazines making fun of Midwestern states" although the article pointed out our low crime rate, good schools, clean air, and low housing costs, concluding that North Dakota might be a good place to move to. But that headline of being "necessary," meant to attract attention, attracted attention, getting a lot of talk around the tables of hometown cafes.

Kathleen Norris, asked about the article, laughed at the elitism of economic theorizers in the East, those who planned unsustainable towns every seven miles along the railroad, who promised rainfall would increase as the land was plowed. But, although our mythology painted us ruggedly independent, we were "remarkably dependent on outside interests." Federal money for our two military bases and agricultural-support programs constituted about 42 percent of the state's economic base and—painful to recognize—the nation probably didn't need as many wheat farmers as it once did, or as many loggers or auto workers. "We may be looking at an era where we have to think small," she said, and perhaps Dakota could lead the way. This might be a good place to figure out how to handle reduction, rather than expansion.

Much of this had been said several years before I sat down beside the windmill and stock tank with even more intensity in the Great North Dakota Buffalo Commons War, still not declared over and still guaranteed to generate the same responses. In 1987, the Poppers—Frank and Deborah, from Rutgers—published a study on the plains, that countryside with about 30 percent of the nation's land mass and 4 percent of its population. Agriculture, ranching, energy, and minerals—the area's main activities—were all economically depressed, true after three historic waves of heavy federal development: the 1862 Homestead Act, starting with atypical rains and ending in widespread starvation; the expansion to 640 acres in the early 1900s and the richness of U.S. wheat in World War I ending in the Dustbowl of the 1930s; and the beginning of large-scale subsidies in the 1940s, encouraging fence-to-fence cultivation and then, in the mid 1980s, busting again.

You could blame the government and eastern interests but there was room to blame those who had "overgrazed and overplowed the land and overdrawn the water." This was taken as impugning the ethics of farmers and ranchers—the best-stewards-of-the-land argument was brought up again and again—but the Poppers thought the situation could hardly be otherwise. Despite our mythology of pioneer effort, the conquering of the plains was actually a system of federally subsidized "privatization," which, given the area's climate and economies, led to unsustainable over-production.

The answer involved "de-privatization," a matter of the government buying people out, the small cities of the plains "urban islands in a short-grass sea," the central plains becoming, they had to say it, a Buffalo Commons, the world's largest historic preservation project. This was, for some Dakotans, fairly easy to visualize as government agents evicting happy citizens from their prosperous ranches and farms and probably wanting to turn it all over to the United Nations.

A year later, the *Grand Forks Herald* interviewed Frank Popper, still recovering from the reaction and wanting to set the record a little straighter. For one thing, he'd picked the buffalo partly for its metaphorical tone—he didn't mean replacing cattle with buffalo—but for another thing, some ranchers *were* starting to raise buffalo. And what had gotten almost lost in the discussion was that the whole theory was much more prediction than plan. The region would continue becoming less populated through the natural workings of economics and climate and the land: that was the given, Popper thought. He was only suggesting how the government could help people cope with the inevitable crisis.

Of course, it still rankled people that some urban professor said their homeland would become "largely empty" and they kept saying it rankled them and their homeland kept emptying. Two years after Popper's *Herald* interview, a national census showed that of the forty-four North Dakota counties beyond the famous 98th meridian—everything west of the Omlid Slough near McVille—forty-one had lost people.

In 1994 the Poppers spoke out again. The subtitle of their first article, "Dust to Dust," had perhaps been too cleverly bleak, and the new one was called "Checkered Past, Hopeful Future." The farming, ranching, energy, and urban development that was economically stable would adjust and remain, but what they'd suggested earlier was already coming true with more local and private-sector initiatives. By this time New Rockford, North Dakota, was the headquarters of the North American Bison Cooperative, which Ted Turner had just joined, and a commercial bison herd munched hay and dozed in the sun only a few miles west of the offices of the *Grand Forks Herald* where editor Mike Jacobs wrote a not unfavorable commentary on Ernest Callenbach's excitedly titled *Bring Back the Buffalo!*

Vine Deloria Jr., writer, professor, and a North Dakota Standing Rock Sioux, thought the Poppers had shown a reality people didn't want to acknowledge—small struggling cities surrounded by vast expanses of open spaces where only large corporate ranching and farming could survive—and a changing future involving a different kind of commerce: buffalo, tourism, hunting preserves. "Once change took place," Deloria said, of the First People who had come onto the land from another way of life, "prosperity ensued. That is a tale told by many Native American tribes in the Great Plains, and it is now the reality that the people of the Great Plains must address."

So we had to look at the local, at who was here. Norris hoped theorists would take into account "the wisdom of those who live here, not only Indians but white ranchers, people who've spent a lifetime on a single ranch and maybe the fourth or fifth generation in their family to do so." Larry Woiwode, a particular fifth-generation North Dakotan, agreed. People had been accumulating experience here for years, and whether they were Norwegian or Native American or German Russian they were all, now, "survivors," dealing with problems other parts of the country would have to face—producing food locally for an increasingly global community. Dakota was "the place where we're going to prove how America, this country, not just this state, is going to be able to survive into the next century."

I sat, humanly alone, in the sunlight in a native grassland beside an icon of plains settlement. People had tried to farm here, had succeeded, had failed. They grazed cattle with permits some said amounted to federal subsidy, the fees less than elsewhere, and others said no, it was marginal land anyway. Some remained and some moved on. Not quite enough soil along the Sheyenne to farm, but we had grazers. Not enough forest to log, but we had tree farmers. In these mixed grasslands, we lived in perpetual transition.

It was past noon so I needed to get to the next location on the map, a crossing at Ironwood Creek, and turn back. Walking through the waving grasses getting ready to seed themselves millions of shimmering times, the slight breeze cooler in a small grove of oak, hotter in the open stretches, I didn't have much water left when I arrived at Ironwood Creek.

In a deep ravine of oak, ash, elm—and ironwood, I supposed—the stream, about five feet across and only inches deep, curled toward the Sheyenne somewhere off in its own trees. The horse trail gouged deeply down the bank and up the other side, but the sandy creekbed was as firmly rippled as if no one had crossed in a year. I moved upstream, studying the ribbed scallops, then took off my boots and socks, gently touched my bare feet down onto the furrows of the bed—a splash of coolness—and lifted them up. Grains of sand whirled from the destroyed terrace, a small cloud of chaos, but another terrace started to form and, within two or three seconds, was furrowed as perfectly as it had been before, the same way or not, impossible to tell.

The cooler my feet, the hotter the rest of my body felt, and I decided on an indulgence. I could hear anyone approaching along the trail and this would be something to remember, a secret I didn't plan then on revealing. I quickly stripped, laid my clothes on the bank, and lowered myself into the shallow chilly water, my skin tightening, a gasp from deep in my lungs, until I half-sat, half-lay on the firm sand of ancient glacial floods and let the creek curve around me, making new furrows and ribs and dunes under the water the color of air. After a few moments, I lay completely back, my head on the sandy bottom arched to keep my nose above the surface. I wasn't Thoreau up to his neck in a bog, but I was close, an old bare log stranded in the middle of a small current.

When I stood up, I looked down at my imprint on the creek bottom, shadowy swirls of dark sand drifting and colliding, and by the time I was up on the bank I couldn't identify where I'd been lying—the creek the familiar shape it had held for centuries, the scallops of snow across a North Dakota field in winter, the curve and cut of desert dunes, the pattern of sandy grasslands if viewed from a sufficient height. If rivers were an "expression" of gravity, maybe all phenomena were such expressions. The grasslands were an expression of wind and water and land, the grasses themselves trillions of singular expressions of one commandment, the oaks and the red-tinged leaves of sumac also expressions, and everyone in Leonard, including Lester and Leila, including the living and the newly dead, along with the Knutsons and the Bergs, Pegleg Nelson and Fisher Olson, the Cheyenne on their long, looping journey across the grassland—all expressions of their various gravities.

The August breeze almost immediately dried me, and I dressed and started back into the heat of the grass. I came onto a bluff that overlooked the Sheyenne and saw only the rounded humps of trees rising up from its water and concealing it, the grassland where people could momentarily lose themselves or spend their lives or try to spend their lives. I spotted a marker and turned east, the little Ironwood Creek behind me which—regardless of punishing trail-rides or the occasional walker or, someday perhaps, of the buffalo—collected itself together again and again in the old way, all the earth an expression of something, and we ourselves along with it.

river end: the bonanza valley

Late fall, I returned almost to Leonard to follow the Sheyenne downstream where it would lose its name to the Red River of the North. Cass County holds North Dakota's highest concentration of people, about sixty per square mile—primarily due to Fargo, the state's largest city—and all of these square miles seem so plainly level they prompt the question, what in the world could *be* this flat? And the answer is a lake, another expression of gravity, every grain of sand or silt or clay settling under the weight of its equal response. A huge cold water—the largest on the ice age continent—had spread from North Dakota up to the last beach of Canada's Lake Winnipeg, named later in its absence for Louis Agassiz, the father of glacial geology for whom natural objects were "thoughts of God." For centuries, Lake Agassiz spread its large flat surface to make a large flat bed, a stability I called home that had formed within a history of fluctuation.

About twelve thousand years ago, glaciers blocked the north-running rivers and streams that gathered into a depth. When glaciers retreated, it drained away northward and when they advanced it rose again, a gigantic intake and outflow of respiration built shore stepping upon shore, beaches you feel as your car rises up east or west of the Red. At the final retreat of ice, the water took a last long breath and left to the north.

For a thousand years, deep forests thrived to be replaced, as the climate changed, by marsh replaced by medium grasses replaced by the tallest of grasses four thousand years ago, dry warm times a little wetter, a little colder, our current conditions. It is difficult for us to live with that perspective. At the most, we base our lives on the importance of a hundred years, which holds together three generations, priding ourselves on the endurance of century farms, celebrating our town's centennial. But the earth is not our ordinary dimension, not even the broad lakebed of the Red River Valley. It seems as though we've made it ours, plowed and planted and harvested it, sunk wells, built towns, turned the rocks of ages into fill for new subdivisions, but it extends and endures on a scale we've never been able to completely comprehend, in our control, out of it again.

There are things we can measure, of course. We know the Red and Sheyenne drop about a foot and a half a mile. We know the Valley tends not to drain well, due partly to topography and partly to its earth. Our fields are either those soil associations called Fargo or Hegne or a mixture, both silty clays, black, then gray, then dark gray brown, the lake plain a silty clay going fifty feet down, then eighty or more of a silty plastic clay, soils suited for how we use them, small grains, soybeans, sunflowers, sugar beets, and potatoes.

We also know there are variations in the flatness, however difficult to see. From a low-flying airplane, Bluemle promises, we'd find the central Valley marked by huge grooves—up to six miles long, a hundred feet wide, three to ten feet deep—which were made, he theorizes, by the lake's icebergs blown by the prevailing wind during spring breakup. The evidence on the ground is in the stretches of planted trees along the fields, tall alternating with short—"beaded shelterbelts," Bluemle calls them—their growth controlled by the differences in soil fertility between the plains and grooves.

So the Valley extended uniformly and varied, a flatness familiar as a backyard or strange as a wilderness and although it could feel crowded—shoppers jostling through a Fargo mall or the harvest bustle of a small town where trucks lined up along the elevators—it could also be a landscape almost eerily empty. Rivers, churches, towns, cemeteries, subdivisions—they existed in the Valley as if only temporary, held between being here and not being here.

I drove north through Kindred, a Great Northern town on the site of an old post office called Sibley, and to the east found the Sheyenne meandering in a tangle of gray-green foliage. When I noticed a graveyard beside the road, a few stones on a tiny lawn separated from the fields only by lilacs and two large spruce trees, I stopped. "Clemson Cemetery," the sign said, the property of that single family, and I read the stones of Henrick and Bertha, both born in the first quarter of the 1800s, both living into the 1900s, century-spanning lives. The fields beyond had given up their crops for this year, the roots of the family's last lawn reaching down only a few feet into the silty clay of the Fargo-Hegne soil.

Five miles farther, I came to Horace, an 1882 Northern Pacific town named for the Mr. Greeley who had said "Go west, young man, and grow up with the country," which right now was appropriate for Horace, its current high population of 650 the effect of Fargo out-migration. I drove past permanent trailers on the south end of town, past a sign for "Bedrooms," and down the main street called Main Street—the Horace Supply, a garage, and a grocery store. The Sheyenne Bar looked sealed up with its plywood door but a neon beer sign glowed in the window; the Horace Lutheran Church announced its founding in 1877. Outside of town, where Main Street turned back into highway, a truck had spilled some wheat as it turned toward the elevator, a trail of hard reddish kernels sown in a perfect semi-circle across the asphalt.

A mile out of Horace, I stopped at another family plot, the Brink Cemetery, Christian from 1845–1920 and Karen from 1833 to 1921, more spanning of the century, then drove past Westwood Addition and Woodland Acres and another string of trailer houses. Near the next bridge lay a road-killed fox close to a sign—"Lots for Sale." I slowed at a newly built house, its yard bare dirt, tender saplings in front although behind it reared a tattered shelterbelt of old cottonwood and ash, the fresh sign in front advertising "Windsor Green Estates."

Now I was nearing Fargo—The Crossing, at first, or Tent City or Centralia—keeping the Sheyenne in sight to the east, a gray water in a controlled channel, and crossed a gravel road where a large sign foretold: "Future Arterial Road/High Volume Traffic/Limited Access." Beyond that, two surveyors were setting up their equipment beside a concrete canal, a diversion project, they explained, to re-route some Sheyenne water around West Fargo during floods and back into the river again at Harwood. One of the surveyors lived in West Fargo and *he'd* never had any flooding and he'd had to pay an extra three hundred dollars in taxes. "For this," he said, gesturing to the concrete channel.

Coming into town, I turned east to stop at Elmwood Park and walk across the lawn to the riverbank. Two or three trees had toppled over, their roots combining by this time into a small island of grass. The current was surely pushing north but the breeze came out of Canada, ruffling the little ripples south, giving the impression of flowing the opposite way.

I stood on the bank almost embarrassed, after everything I'd seen of the river, at what it was reduced to, the backyard stream of a dozen or so houses before it disappeared around a curve. In the mud-plastered undergrowth of weeds across from me lay the coil of a green hose, a couple of plastic bottles, a yellowed newspaper still folded, unread and decaying, the usual plastic sack rattling in a bush. In one yard, a dilapidated treehouse clung to its perch, a few weathered boards nailed to the trunk so many years ago its builder would be grown by now. In another yard, a metal pole held a fluttering U.S. flag claiming the back view of a river lot in the name of my country.

The sun starting to slant over the last of the harvest, I curved past Fargo—thriving cities were not my concern—and headed north, still thinking about living in two centuries, about Christian and Karen Brinks, Henrik and Bertha Clemenson. In what way *had* they done something like "bridge" two different times? Or my own grandfathers, now that I thought of it? Or, now that I'd really thought of it, what would it mean for me to do so, looking toward the next millennium? Maybe the important century was not the one ending or beginning on New Year's Eve in 1900, but that century that ended with the farm crises of the 1980s and began with the Valley's bonanza farms of the 1880s. The sound of that word was an important echo for life in the Valley. It may have meant something like "fair weather" in the vulgar Latin, may have come from *bonus*, the root of our words for bounty and beneficence and beauty and benefit, but it stood as a resounding definition of those times we made an immensity of land our own. More or less.

Bonanza Country. By the 1870s, Minneapolis was the nation's largest milling center and Dakota was close by with its large tracts of Northern Pacific land and its attractive failures, the homesteads of the unsuccessful up for sale. In the first five years of the decade, the Valley's population doubled, cultivated land increasing sixfold. Wheat prices were inflated by the effects of the Civil War, so it was good to grow it but production costs were also high so large scale production was a possible answer.

The first true bonanza farm—3,000 acres the minimum to meet this description—was the Dalrymple in 1876, owned by George Washington Cass, President of the Northern Pacific, who, wanting to demonstrate the value of railroad land for large holders, established an agricultural model of assembly-line efficiency. In a few years the Dalyrimple farm—divided into units of 500 acres, each with its own house, barn, and other facilities—employed 400 men in the harvest rush, working with 115 self-binding harvesters, 100 broadcast seeders, and 400 horses and mules.

Boom and Rush. In the spring of 1883, immigration reached five thousand in one day. Passenger trains were full of "comers and lookers," as the Fargo *Argus* put it, and hotels filled, cots lining hallways and crammed together in parlors, rooms blanketed off into smaller rooms. The famous farms stretched and swelled, ninety-one of them in the Valley. James Powers, successful in selling Northern Pacific land and now doing the same for Jim Hill's line, promised in his pamphlets a land "rich beyond all comparison in soil, healthful in climate, and blessed with a population of unsurpassed intelligence, energy, enterprise, and hospitality."

Into this blessed land came Mary Dodge Woodward, her introduction an inscription on a passing wagon: "Dakota—the poor man's friend, the world's granary." Living on what became a bonanza farm, she kept a journal from 1884 to 1889, writing of what was around her and thus of what is here almost a century later and what is forever missing.

I'd been struck by her feel of the surrounding space. Although men swelled the hotels of towns, there was a loneliness about the open countryside. "There's no road at all between here and Fargo," she wrote shortly after her arrival, "and some of the way the boys could not see one light." It was easy to understand, she thought, how people became lost on this "boundless sea of undulating land," quoting a newspaper she'd read. A couple of days later she recorded that Mr. McAuliffe, a resident for seven years, had gotten lost coming home at night and rescued himself by finally blundering into a haystack and—luckier than Rolvaag's Per Hansa—finding the path to a neighbor's house.

The Valley's history, of course, is the filling of that space, and Woodward, often using a spyglass, could observe schoolhouses being built, could ultimately discern a hundred farmhouses. "Who would have believed," she wrote, "that seven years ago there was not a cabin on the prairie."

The expanse of the level Valley made any weather seem universal, an Everything, a Nothing, and this was especially true of winter. It's unfair that winter is the season that often first comes to mind at the mention of North Dakota, but North Dakota winters are frequently impressive. James Powers assured his readers that Dakota blizzards served to remove "all miasma and contagion" from the fields and valleys and "breathe new life into dilapidated nostrils," but the winters were rough in several ways. Mary Woodward felt a powerful physical effect—"The snow has fallen all day in a blinding mass, piling into drifts and striking the house with such force that it fairly trembled"—but also a psychological effect. "When we look out," she wrote, "it is like gazing into an eternal empty space. It gives me a homesick feeling as though I were shut out from everyone except those in the house." Eternal, again. Empty, again.

She recorded the winter stories of being lost and being saved or not. She tallied the sixty frozen corpses found left after one year's winter and she joined the territory's anguish over the sudden and infamous January 1888 blizzard in which scores of Dakota schoolchildren died. Closer to home, she wrote of neighbor Eric Johnson, trapped in a storm with his stranded and exhausted cattle. Helpless in the deepening drifts with night coming on, he watched as a large ox "became bewildered and lay down in the snow to die," then killed the ox, gutted it, and crawled inside for protection. In the morning, the carcass having frozen, he was reduced to muffled shouts until a neighbor came to help him escape the night's bloody shelter.

Spring returned, of course, to the bonanza farms, but each season's weather still controlled the land. In April, she wrote, "Everything is mud, and *such* mud, black and heavy and sticky like glue. Nobody can imagine what Dakota mud is like until he gets into it and tries to lift his feet." In May, "The wind blows all the time so hard that one can scarcely stand it. We cannot open the front door for if we should, this room would soon be empty." And, on another spring day, "Fog flies in the air almost like snow and one might as well be on the boundless ocean for all one can see." Later, the earth drying, her boys could hardly see to plow in a blasting of dust—"They said all the soil seemed to be in the air at once."

But if bad times seemed to be universal in this large land, so did the good: "How beautiful the wheat fields look," she wrote one harvest time, "long avenues between the shocks, just as straight, one mile in length." It was amazing—"The whole of Cass County was covered with No. 1 Hard Wheat, and the wayside was all abloom with goldenrod and asters."

Attracted to this richness, men flooded in, the country "alive with teams, seeding and dragging," but not all arriving workers were the prairie yeomen of our American imagination. "The country is full of men tramping about," she wrote one July, "and begging at farm houses as they stop to hire out." They had found three tramps outside whom they allowed to sleep in the barn but in general Woodward thought they were fortunate to live far from the railroad tracks where such men went by the elevators in droves.

Our forebears in the Valley, pioneers and wanderers, entrepreneurs and tramps, did not solve the exact relationship of humans to their work. Nor have we, for all of that, with our unsupported nostalgia for the small family farms of the past and our unsupported faith in the corporations that make the future inevitable and call it progress. We're not quite sure how we make a home for ourselves here. The bonanza operations did not give rise to what we think of as rural communities because their seasonal employment attracted mainly migrant labor. Now, threshing crews still move through and migrant workers, their skins usually a shade darker than the fair complexions of the Norwegian, chop weeds in the potato and sugar beet fields, sometimes accepted, sometimes not, and sometimes all but invisible.

There was another shadow in the old valley. Small towns and rural areas claim a friendly neighborliness as one of their main virtues, yet Woodward observed that "Nobody keeps track of his neighbors here. People come and go, families move in and out, and nobody asks whence they came nor whither they go." Traveling to a farm a mile and a half away to inquire about the use of a well, they discovered that the owner had died six months before. Not our usual view of rural adhesiveness or pioneer cooperation: "I have lived here six years and I do not know who occupies half of the surrounding farms although they are in full view."

While whole families moved in and out at the edge of Woodward's knowledge, history moved through and past. In April 1884, she noted that Sitting Bull had come through Fargo on his way to St. Paul and that he "looks to be failing." Dressed in a greasy hunting suit, his face a mass of wrinkles, he appeared "little like the great warrior history will portray." In late August she quoted the *Argus* story that someone had tried to assassinate him in St. Paul—"People say he would lead his braves on the warpath at the slightest provocation," she worried. Instead, from his cabin on the Grand River in southern Dakota where he grew vegetables and raised cattle, he joined the Buffalo Bill Cody tour in 1885.

Dakota Territory separated officially into North and South in 1889, two years after the Dawes' Allotment Act brought the lonely order of homestead to the Sioux, opening up what the *wasichu* considered "surplus" land, and one year before the Ghost Dance religion with its rumors of a new messiah attracted Sitting Bull's attention enough for Agent McLaughlin to authorize his arrest. When Indian police arrived, a series of blunders escalated, the police pushing from one side, relatives and supporters from the other, until there was gunfire, Sitting Bull dead, police dead, friends, relatives, his fourteen-year-old son.

That year, 1890, growing frail, Mary Dodge Woodward was transported from the Dakota frontier back to Wisconsin where she died, her own era ending, a small story almost lost but for her words in the magnitude of the Valley. Yet bonanza farming was never a complete reality, the huge farms never dominating, the average size across the state in 1890 less than 300 acres. Something was draining away. The First Dakota Boom had stimulated small farmers to enlarge their holdings as it advertised the new country's potential to outsiders, but much was fueled by speculation. Wheat prices had started down as early as 1873 and kept sliding, a stream of potential drying up at the same time people poured in. These "market conditions," as economists call them, accounted for the migrations out of North Dakota soon after settlement, the rush in and the rush out.

There was a Second Dakota Boom from 1898 until World War I, more or less a reflection of national trends, but something had finished here, a wave had fallen back. The pioneers had done too well, "The Too-Much Mistake" of Elwyn Robinson, by building a society with too many institutions and not enough people. By 1910, settlement practically completed, the Mid-Atlantic states held 193 people per square mile and Ohio 117. The Valley had sixteen and North Dakota's average was eight. This was the year of peak population in town after town across this harvested landscape.

Still, some were here to stay and by the 1920s agriculture in the Valley had "matured," if by that we mean about the same pattern we're familiar with. We have a harvest every year, one-sixth of the total U.S. wheat, more than 600 bushels for each North Dakotan, thank you. After "flamboyant exploitation"—this is how Dakota historian Stan Murray sees it—our agriculture entered a period of "patient experimentation." Still, no matter how improved the seed or the science, we continue to live within the fluctuations of abundance and shortage because that *is* the Valley, and close to forever, the rhythms of rise and fall in fields that hold all harvest, under a sky that holds all summer in its reach and then all winter Everywhere.

Late afternoon, I turned east off the Interstate near Harwood—an 1880 Great Northern town, its population of six hundred an 81 percent increase in the last decade, more out-migration from Fargo—and drove past the weight of dark grain elevators, following the Sheyenne's channeled ditch, toward Section 13 of Harwood Township where it would disappear.

I was only a few miles away but when I found the long driveway of the Osterdalen—for "eastern valley"—Lutheran Church, 1887, I couldn't resist stopping. Walking among the stones, I found other lives bridging the centuries, like Gjermund Nyum who was born the year before Nicollet passed through the surrounding countryside and died the year before the U.S. entered World War II. Then I came to Karl Ostby, 1862 to 1957, born the year of the Sioux Uprising, seventy-five years old when I was born, and dying two years after I graduated from high school.

This sudden intrusion of history on my own life made me stand there longer than usual until a farmer wheeled his pickup alongside the cemetery and got out. He'd seen me come up to the church—lived over there, he nodded—and could he help? I said I was trying to find where the Sheyenne entered the Red and he pointed to the next driveway down, but didn't I want to see the church? They'd spent a lot of time preserving and reconstructing it. He unlocked the door and we entered, one usher with one stranger, so he could proudly point out the windows, the polished floors, the shining pews and fixtures the way Lester had shown me his church one county down. The Osterdahl Settlement, he said, had been a rural community of Norwegians from Iowa. The church smelled of wood and hymn books and the old-fashioned sanctity of a small congregation who raised the point of their Lutheran spire against the eternal weathers of the prairie.

We parted at the end of the driveway, and I took the next one up to a brick, ranch-style house. When no one answered I walked around to the barn, now a fabric shop named "Country Designs," and I opened the door to the scents of fresh lumber and the acidic tang of new carpeting. A woman talking on the phone held her hand over the mouthpiece and lifted her eyebrows in question, eyebrows which didn't react at all when I told her what I'd come to see. Second-floor, she mouthed, pointing to the stairs as if I'd asked to see her inventory, and returned to her conversation, setting something straight, no, she already told her that, no, that wouldn't work. And then I was standing at the upstairs window, looking out at the small ending of an ancient waterway.

I could tell last spring's rise from the high-watered straw and gray tatters of plastic, knew that the trees had stood in swirls of dark water and that I couldn't have distinguished Red from Sheyenne from flooded woodland. Last spring, it was no doubt the mirror of its confused origin, a swollen gathering and dispersal of waters, but now it had shrunk to a ditch winding through the woods. A swirl of silty water curled into the siltier water of the Red, one name here, another there.

Because this was Section 13, across from me must have been the site of old Georgetown, Minnesota, where Hudson Bay goods from St. Paul were first transferred to the river and, somewhere south on this side, was the site of Dakota City, a settlement abandoned after the 1862 Uprising. I stood at the window a moment or two longer, looking at the little flux below me, waters that had risen near the James only to separate from it, "emblematic of the course pursued by many families of the human race" as the Wells County history had said. I wanted to see more than I was seeing and knew I was seeing less than what there was. Finally I came back down the stairs, thanked the owner and left the new Country Designs, the old Dakota City, and the important and insignificant departure of what I'd come to think of as "my river." I had traced a course through what we call history and what we call our lives, trying to contain ourselves in the boxes of past and present, but something was always moving, "newer waters," as Heraclitus may have said.

Sometimes I get purposely lost, trying to find out something about where I am by not knowing where I am. Heading north, although it was getting late, I impulsively turned off the interstate at Grandin—another Great Northern 1880 townsite, John Grandin another bonanza farmer of the Valley—and turned east on a dirt road, south on another. Finally I had no idea where I was except on earth, the half-light of the sky like winter, the fields like frozen waves of brown and tarnished silver. A haze of light bloomed to the south, someone's hometown.

I passed a sign warning "Unimproved Road" and bumped on through the gouges of broad heavy tires or over tractor tracks ribbing the edge. I turned on my lights but it was that half-time of dimness that both illuminates and obscures and I kept misjudging the road, the Escort scraping over a ridge of high dirt in the middle or shaking rhythmically over a hard washboard. Walled by sunflowers, the road became a lane, then two parallel trails, and then it was almost dark. And then it was dark.

From the east, a pair of bright lights swung startlingly into sight, strangely high above the field, and bounced forward, a huge, picker churning past me, the large-headed bodies of sunflowers illuminated in its glare before they disappeared into a rotating blade. I stopped the car, nothing ahead but clod and furrow, gouge and hump, and climbed out to stand on the cold bottom of the empty lake. Behind me, the picker reached the end of its row by the road, swung eastward deep into its harvest, and disappeared.

Mary Woodward had written one fall of someone lost on the foggy prairie near their farm—"We could hear him halloo for two hours." They didn't go to his assistance as there were houses in that direction and it wasn't cold, but they hung out lights, although "it is difficult to see them in a fog," and that was that. I thought of being truly lost where I stood and of whoever it was that hallooed that length of time in that great darkness. I thought of all the others now lost, Mr. Cass of Cass County, Mr. Rich of Richland County, Mr. Fargo of Fargo, Mr. Kindred of Kindred, Mr. Harwood of Harwood, Mr. Gardner of Gardner, Mr. Grandin of Grandin. And of Karl Ostby, dying in my lifetime and now in the Osterdalen cemetery, of Henrik and Bertha, of Christian and Karen. Giants over the earth and inside the earth.

I stood alone in the gigantic factory of food that runs at night, perhaps all night this season, with its Boom, its Boom, its Bonanza.

South of me, the Sheyenne was emptying itself through a little scratch of woods into a larger matter over and over. I was, for just this moment, standing in absolute space both filled and emptied, alone and lost among neighbors, my home somewhere out there, one haze of light among others, in the immensity of darkness over an immensity of earth.

the winter houses

The light was mixed that October morning, the sun slant-ing under a dark shelf of clouds as I looked down from my fifth-floor apartment, the street dotted with clods of mud from sugar-beet trucks on their way to the Great Crystal plant in East Grand Forks, here and there the huge lump of a beet itself. Every few years a citizen would write the *Grand Forks Herald* to complain about this and others would reply, explaining the nature of nature in the Valley. And saying something of our own natures as well. "Man is the fate of his place," wrote poet Thom McGrath, "and place the fate of the man," a recurring theme at the center of North America although what exactly it might mean to us, and thus to everyone else, was still being discovered.

My plan was one final journey to the Sheyenne's origin and to the nearby ghost town of Lincoln Valley since Doug Wick's description promised "houses" there. There was an added poignancy because I was changing homes next spring after 23 years of enjoying a Dakota life. Already I'd driven by the house of my first long marriage, left empty a week before new owners arrived so that my son, he later confessed, could sneak in and walk through the small histories of bare rooms, seeing the marks on rugs and floors where the stable furniture of his childhood had stood. I ate breakfast, took the elevator down, walked past the lobby's photographs of steamboats still high and dry, and climbed into the Escort.

To the west lay the extensive farm of John Scott begun by his grandfather John Scott in 1879 who farmed, as he put it, on the nine-hour principle: working nine hours before lunch and nine hours after. His account of early days rang with familiar echoes. The land was unobstructed prairie, not a tree or shrub between the Turtle and the Forest Rivers the next county north with no landmarks so that once he and a neighbor left a claim shack in a thick Dakota mist, driving the wagon for hours until they should have reached the Turtle River, stopping at night by two haystacks that looked familiar, realizing they had driven all afternoon to arrive back half a mile from the claim shack. This is a quintessential prairie story, true every time we tell it, shaking our heads helplessly at how we are kept from our destinations by snow or fog or darkness. We spend time founding a home, and then some time losing ourselves in the space around it. But John did build a heritage for the Scotts to come, showing one way people could make a home here, first enduring and then thriving.

I passed through Thompson—train station and farm-town in

1880, farm-town and bedroom-community to Grand Forks now, its population tripling in the last twenty years to a thousand—between old and new, a suburb one block back from the highway, on the right a ragged wood home with no sidewalk, on the left a brick house with freshly white gazebo and formal garden, more change in the middle of what seemed never to change.

In what ways *did* our place became our fate? Elwyn Robinson thinks our remoteness emphasizes the virtues of courage and friendliness, the climate helping to make us a hustling, energetic people. For historian David Danbom, we exemplify the usual values of a rural past coupled with material scarcity: independence, hard work, neighborliness, and mutual help. South Dakota poet John Milton believes our climate makes us friendly, spiritually expansive.

But the plains have shadowed our nature as well. Our exploitation by outside interests, says Robinson, has made us suspiciously independent, loyal members of a self-conscious minority. For Danbom, our position on the periphery makes social problems such as crime or environmental degradation less apparent, which can give rise to a certain smug self-satisfaction. Yet we are controlled by and dependent upon the "outside," so much a colony in the hinterland that we are unsure of our own worth. We have, put bluntly, a fierce sense of independence and an inferiority complex simultaneously. We are, it seems, a people of conflicting characteristics—loyal and suspicious, slow to anger and quickly dismissive, expansive and narrow, the sunlight of the open prairie and the shadows of lives lived in cramped quarters, which determined not only how we viewed ourselves but how we looked at others, making our towns in the same image of tension.

Larry Woiwode credits the extremes of pioneer experience for the sense of survivorship he finds still strong and for the acceptance of diversity in the smallest community. Kathleen Norris thinks the landscape may have made us acceptingly tolerant, that people "totally dependent on a harsh, unforgiving land" often came to learn the lessons of forgiving, developing a "fairly sophisticated ethic of 'Live and let live'" and I've found that to be true.

But there is another side. Milton admits we are "beset with rural and small-town prejudices, racial prejudice, provincialism." Norris experienced neighbor-helping-neighbor but, as well, the "fault line of suspicion and divisiveness exposed by the farm crisis in the mid-1980s," which left wounds in her community not yet healed.

Last summer, a university institute released its Rural Life survey, the *Herald* headline "Poll Paints Glum Picture of Rural Life." There were high rates of rural unemployment—18 percent of farmers, 27 percent of non-farmers—and some said the biggest threat to rural North Dakota was a lack of jobs but three-quarters said low wages. Asked if people depended on each other as they once did, 88 percent said no, no, no. About a third thought their community was closely knit and about a third disagreed with them. Yet in spite of these results, the respondents scored below the midpoint on stress and anxiety. This was the news, according to the institute's director. He had expected higher stress levels among people whose economic security often depended on things beyond their control, the fate of our place. He guessed it was like a continual condition. "You get used to it after a while," he said. "It's like a chronic back pain."

I turned south to Hatton, the highway becoming Dakota Avenue, and drove past the cemetery where Carl Ben Eielson was buried. Born nearby—the world, wherever one looked, three-quarters sky— Eielson left one remoteness for another by becoming a pilot in Alaska in the early 1920s. Trading the long Dakota winter for the longer Arctic night, he explored in a few years more of the northern skies than anyone had and died in 1929 on a rescue mission in Siberia, the final degree of remoteness.

Hatton was also the home of the Country Squire Inn, which, the next year, would be closed up by Jean and Tilford Thompson, the farewell party covered by the *Herald*, the Thompson kids thanking the newspaper and paying tribute to their parents for fifty-three years' faithful service to the Hatton area. "What has taken place in Hatton is felt by anyone in Smalltown USA who has experienced this wonderful quality of life," the Thompson kids said.

Nevertheless, our fates continue in our place. We live in the geography of an apparent forever, roads running through a flow of eternal wheat or sunflowers or sugar beets or grazing land, above us an arch of huge blue space, and when our grandfather and grandmother are buried right over there, we feel an at-homeness in this space. Nevertheless, when a woman in her early thirties tells Norris their town has to get back to what it was twenty years ago, when another hopes a new school superintendent doesn't want to change things and another hopes that of the new minister, we are in trouble. Perhaps, she says, we emulate the land that alters so slowly that it seems not to, but we are in danger of losing the ability to change, which means a diminished capacity for hope.

I thought of all of us as I drove, our small trips and long journeys, nomads even if our family cemetery was nearby, our town the flash of a century old. I thought of the Cheyenne, a people living through one national identity after another.

I drove out of Hatton, its population always less than a thousand, holding people who had left and people who had stayed, Dakota Avenue becoming highway again, and passed a young girl straddling her bicycle in a farm driveway. She waved, and I waved back, watching her in the rearview mirror, still on her bicycle, not moving, smaller and smaller.

I turned up north on Highway 45 to cross the Sheyenne on the bridge I'd never gotten to in my canoe, the open water on both sides still hiding its impenetrable logjams, and drove through Aneta, my conservative friend probably in the cafe this morning worrying about the end of America. The town's centennial would be next year, and so would Sharon's, Finley's the year after that, all three along the Great Northern railroad spur, a hundred-year clock striking, the ghost of history past, of history to come. The clouds had settled in again, looking like rain, more moisture Devils Lake didn't need, and I turned west just before McVille—*Mack*-ville—taking a gravel road and coming to the bridge where a few weeks ago I'd fallen into the Sheyenne and discovered at least one secret of life.

I'd persuaded Ike, a biologist friend, to help me with his expertise as well as his hip boots and seine net. Fishermen here caught Northern Pike or Yellow Perch, but I was more interested in the tiny exotica of Ike's specialty, what would to me be hidden. We arrived at what he called "a low-gradient prairie stream with fine and unstable substrates" and seined the water bank to bank, finding nothing, and trying for nothing again. Too late in the year, Ike guessed. During one more sweep I felt the surprise of rocks along the soft bottom and the moment Ike said "Be careful of the rocks," my foot slipped and I lurched to stand and slipped more, my boots filling as I slid into the cold water, my lungs tightening at the shock. Confused by the current's surprising pull and the growing weight of my boots, I thrashed and floundered for a footing until I finally gave up and clumsily swam the three strokes to the bank.

While I dried off, Ike brought up one of those very rocks, the underside crusted with tiny pebbly knobs, the retreats of caddis fly larvae. This time of year, each tiny worm, the first stage in a family of four-winged insects, took whatever was around it— grains of sand, shell bits, fragments of sticks—and patched together a cylinder where it lived for a season, a house allowing the water's nutrients to flow through and collect. Today I crossed the bridge—knowing the thousands of intricately pebbled retreats hidden below me, their inhabitants waiting out the long months of winter in a continual current—and then turned up toward the highway.

I'd asked Ike on the way home about the stability or instability of the Sheyenne he'd seen. Well, the important concept to remember in geomorphology—I did some quick Latin translation to get to *earth* and *form*—was "dynamic equilibrium." Some things were predictable—the relationship between square miles of drainage and the amount of flow in a stream, for example—but there was also change in erosion and deposition, which influenced that relationship. The finer the detail, he said, the more difficult prediction is, and here we were again, I thought, living by fine daily detail, working the land while living with weather, against the cycle of a decade, a century, the inhuman perspective of a few thousand years.

I cruised past Hamar, wondering if the bar owner was still the man who'd found the bones of a monster in his field, and through Sheyenne where the restaurant was closed—due to illness, said a sign in the window—and continued heading west but also West, a way of life from which something had sprung. In 1861, while Captain Fisk led a gold train through Dakota and the waters of the Minnesota Uprising gathered and swelled, Frederick Turner was born, the historian who would, at thirty-two, deliver his famous thesis. Unfairly condensed: free land—toward which flocked hunters, traders, miners, pioneer farmers, and city dwellers—was a frontier that had caused and preserved the American Virtues of Progress, Democracy, and Individualism.

He gave the speech in 1893, and it took awhile for us to accept his thesis, awhile to be overwhelmed by it, and awhile to attack it: the "free" land not as important as he'd thought, the frontier less a safety valve for discontented eastern workers than the next step by sons of farmers, the West not an escape from economic woes since most moved in more prosperous times when they had money. And he'd certainly omitted from his parade of American types the omnipresent land-speculator, doctors, lawyers, and shopkeepers, in a frenzy of Guess and Bet, Boom and Fall.

But even if Democracy or Individualism had not originated on the frontier, each American characteristic, as Ray Allen Billington pointed out mid-century, was deepened and sharpened by frontier conditions and his descriptions of the tensions in our national character sounded about right: democracy and isolationism, pride and arrogance, a practical ingenuity and indifference toward intellectualism and aesthetic values. These were, he says, pioneer traits, and they were traits in North Dakota, and they were—for better and for worse, until death parted us all—our national heritage.

So I traveled West, the frontier vanishing in front of me—the 98th parallel through the Omlid Slough and Valley City, the 99th about a mile east of Sheyenne and close to Ft. Totten, the 100th along the west edge of Harvey, about at the end of Pony Gulch, maybe cutting across the suicide's grave of Mrs. Coff who could take no more. And yet the frontier all around me, wherever the annual rainfall lessened to semi-arid, the grass grew shorter, and the winter had more of an edge to its wind, wherever we'd moved with an optimism born out of wet years, living our lives as if God were good weather always. We thought it would last, we even thought it would get better. Then we learned different, and we learned it again.

Turner died in 1932 and four years later—the year of North Dakota's highest population and number of farms—the president's Great Plains Committee reported that the plains had baffled its people for centuries, agriculture failing to adapt itself to a cycle that included drought. The fluctuation of rainfall didn't even need to be as great as other parts of the country—our weather was important in a way not paralleled elsewhere and we hadn't taken that into account.

The committee also criticized our so-called Rugged Individualism. "The Plainsman cannot assume," the Committee warned, "that whatever is for his immediate good is also good for everybody, nor can he assume the right always to do with his own property as he likes—he may ruin another man's property if he does." Thus, it was officially recognized that we are dependent on each other and cannot conquer Nature.

It wasn't the first time we'd heard this. In 1909—the Second Dakota Boom coming to an end, the Martins and Nehers heading into their winter in a boxcar—Roosevelt's Commission on Country Life told the Senate that generations of training had made the typical plains citizen a strong individualist who did not recognize the importance of cooperation for business purposes or social objectives. Jonathan Raban, in *An American Romance,* attacks this as a "classic text of Progressivism," an excuse for the government to socialize and subdue the independent farmer, but the conclusion of the 1936 commission was an admission that the Great Plains "have not responded favorably to a purely individualistic system of pioneers." It was, however, confident a system could be found to invoke the power of voluntary cooperation without sacrificing local initiative and self-reliance and, as a matter of fact, a substantial part of North Dakota's history developed as just such a cooperative progressivism. Sixty years later, we were still working on that, from the North Dakota State Bank and State Mill to the Farmers Coop to bison cooperatives and ostrich associations.

"In a sense," the Commission wrote, "the Great Plains afford a test of American ways of dealing with matters of urgent common concern," and this special position of Dakota has been often emphasized by Norris, Woiwode, and others. Here, they are saying, is where something happened, and where something will happen, that America should study. When the frontier closed, or whatever it did, America came of age, recognizing, says Harold Simonson, "that limitation is a fundamental fact of life." We will have to learn to live with less, and it is on these Dakota grounds that we may first be tested. We are remembering what we learned before and trying to imagine what we'll need later to have a home on this land.

Late that day, a couple hundred miles from home, I came into Sheridan County on a gravel road and then turned onto a field road heading to Krueger Lake. Soon I stood on the pebbly shoreline. It was chilly and wet now, clouds lying against the ground, strangely like last spring, little stings of ice against my face as I searched for the southern tip, the thin line of the Sheyenne seeping away. I thought I saw it, but it was too distant for a walk. The lake was the lesson now, named for an early German-Russian resident, its waters traceable at least as far back as the glaciers, as far away, cold wavelets in a gouged hollow of land. Who, indeed, could live here? The *scape* in "landscape" comes from an old sound for scraping away and I was standing in a place cut out by ice and ice-driven rock and wind-driven water. "Last night. This morning. The rock and the wind," Thom McGrath wrote on the Greek island of Skyros: "North Dakota is everywhere." Theseus dead like Crazy Horse, the dialectic of poverty and money everywhere as it was in North Dakota, the wind scraping over the rock everywhere as well. This scoop of lake in the undulating prairie was one more example of what I'd found all summer, the permanence of transition, something new lapping along the stony shore, something ancient swelling in the middle. Then I walked back, blinking against the grit of light rain.

Turner presented his famous thesis at the Historical Conference at the 1893 World's Columbian Exposition at Chicago, itself a centennial city that year, a carnival of conflicting culture into which ultimately poured almost 10 percent of the U.S. population. It was a pure White City, an attempt, it's been said, to counterbalance 1890s American materialism, confused traditional values, and economic and social dislocation, with a healthy dose of American idealism and art and social responsibility. Much of it was built on an 82-acre island of dredged-up sand and we know the old warning about *that*.

At the main entrance rose a golden Renaissance dome of Grandeur and Order although at least as many people entered through the Midway of Entertainment, the other version of America. Here two gigantic wheels, the first appearance of George Washington Ferris' machine, carried two thousand people on a complete revolution every ten minutes, overlooking an artificial Streets of Cairo, models of St. Peters and the Eiffel Tower, an imitation Hawaiian volcano, a fake Colorado gold mine.

It was everything we were: Paderewsky and Scott Joplin, John Dewey and Clarence Darrow, Samuel Gompers and Henry Adams, and an international beauty show, "40 Ladies from 40 Countries." It was Buffalo Bill's show and it was Sitting Bull's cabin, dismantled in South Dakota and reassembled here—"War Dances Given Daily," the sign said. Although the Midway sported "a village from Africa," African Americans had been excluded, Frederick Douglass complained, none appointed to the commission, no jobs other than menial ones. "To the colored people of America," he pointed out, "the World's Fair now in progress is a whited sepulcher."

It was, in short, our American Home, material and ethereal, a gleaming metropolis and a whited sepulcher, built with the frontier values of pride and arrogance into an architecture of wisdom and ignorance. "The Exposition itself denied philosophy," Adams wrote, and I could almost see him shake his head. "One could find fault and criticize and complain until the last gate closed and one could still explain nothing that needed explanation." War Dances Given Daily. Forty Ladies from Forty Countries.

In the Philosophy Conference, James Skelton paralleled Turner's thesis, announcing the westward march of empire over and the beginning of a new epoch in which the race would again be tested. The first test soon arrived. In the summer and fall of the Panic of 1893, thousands of workers were left unemployed. By winter, ragged and homeless men were moving back toward the east, "fierce of aspect and terrifying to the people of the hamlets and sparsely settled districts through which they passed," as contemporary Francis Halsey described it. "You look like Coxey's Army," my father's mother would remark if I was dirty or unkempt, comparing me to these men that Jacob S. Coxey attempted to organize into the "The Army of the Commonweal of Christ" to march on Washington.

That winter, the abandoned White City—much of it only facade, the buildings too costly to maintain—became a series of shelters inhabited by vagrants and Chicago's dislocated poor. The next summer, the railroad workers went on strike nearby and General Miles, the previous Grand Marshal of the Exposition, led federal troops against them. In the melee, the last great buildings erupted in flame, the fantasy city founded on sand reduced in two hours to charred girders and drifts of ashes. Sitting Bull was dead as was Mary Dodge Woodward. Rachel Calof had just arrived to marry Abraham near Devil's Lake. Coxey was arrested in Washington mid-speech, only finishing it years later on those same capitol steps, many of his Populist ideas now part of the New Deal, something restless in 1893, something changing. Charlie Johnson was twenty-three years old and North Dakota, as a state, was five.

Krueger Lake lapping behind me in its hollow rock, I turned a few miles north of Denhoff onto a grassy lane lined with a straggly shelter belt of trees and tried to maneuver my way around ruts and holes toward the houses of Lincoln Valley. Grasses whisked under the tires—*Tish-ah,* Rolvaag quoted the grass—and the high-centered glacial dirt scraped the undercarriage until I winced.

George Reiswig sold the site to the Great Northern in 1899, but when the railroad didn't come he bought it back and founded Lincoln in 1900, the year the Calofs' wheat had been destroyed by hail, Charlie Johnson still a clerk in a Wisconsin drugstore but thinking about the West of North Dakota. In 1912 the town became Lincoln Valley, never more than a hundred people. When Joe Lentz, the last remaining man, emptied out his implement store and moved to New Rockford in the early 1970s, a few years after I'd arrived in the state, that was it.

I turned onto the main street, a wide avenue of grass, and cautiously edged past the burned-out remains of the bar on my left, a boarded up church on the right. Several houses still stood, most the flaking color of winter, and I stopped at one with a side door standing open. Inside, I stepped carefully across the torn linoleum, gritty with broken glass and littered with bits of rag, stuffing, and splintered wood, scritching toward what looked like a child's school workbook splayed in the corner. I picked up *Living Today: Health, Safety, Science,* and inside the cover found one word, "Henry."

I squatted down and started reading. Published in 1957—Sheridan County falling from five thousand to four thousand people—it began with a section on farm life, Ann and Billy spending a year on their grandparents' farm. What, the text asked, could Ann and Billy do at the farm that they could not do in the city? And Henry had written "Ride a horse, ride pigs, milk the cow, cultivating, feed the chickens." Ride pigs? I grinned at Henry's lived experience in Lincoln Valley. Sitting now, my back against the cold wall of the abandoned house, my boots scratching on broken glass, I turned the next page: "What vegetables did you eat yesterday?" was answered by "Potatoes, green beans." On the next, "What food made from a bran did you have for breakfast?" and Henry had answered, "Oat meal and toast".

I turned the page but Henry had stopped, only the textbook continuing its questions from 1957, and the room seemed even lonelier with no more answers from the boy who had dutifully, if briefly, done his homework while outside his window the town melted slowly away. I gathered myself up, set the book down gently, and stepped outside.

Stumbling over boards or machinery parts hidden in the tall wet grass, I passed houses weathering away and sidewalks leading only to bush-filled cellars, hollows that, like those of the Cheyenne village, might tell us the dimensions of the lives lived there. I peeked into the charred gape of the bar, then crossed the wide grass to the church, windows boarded, doors locked tight, some-one not allowing the old faith to stain, burn, or fall apart. I circled back to Henry's house, got in my car, took one more look, and left Lincoln Valley, having found enough ghosts for today, the grass whispering whatever it always said.

An icy mist gusted across the highway as I headed north and just before the first bridge over the Sheyenne saw the sign for the Lonetree Wildlife Management Area. Because the little flood last spring had kept me from visiting, and because I had nowhere else to drive but home and didn't really want the journey to end, I turned in.

Lone Tree was the natural lake in the area, Coal Mine and Sheyenne Lakes part of the Garrison Diversion Project to bring more water to North Dakota, a plan in the federal works for years, attacked and defended, bogged down and rescued, for years a booming belief in Garrison almost a requirement for public office. Now the project was mainly Garrison Dam on the Missouri, which backed up what we called Lake Sakakawea, honoring an Indian while flooding Indian land, more than 150,000 acres in 1954 of Fort Berthold—home of the Mandan, Hidatsa, and Arikara—drowning rich farmland and original communities, cutting the reservation into five isolated parts, clans and neighbors split-up and pushed over here, over there, no attempt made to reestablish communities, one of the stresses currently causing the population to decline.

So we conquered the prairie, making lakes out of rivers or rivers out of marshy sloughs, and sometimes the river escaped or the prairie conquered us back. Lonetree, like Lake Tewaukon, had been a wildlife prairie that was homesteaded and farmed and now wildlife again. I stopped at the visitor center, the only visitor, and picked up the brochure for the auto tour, then drove the wet sandy road, a glance at the brochure, a glance out the window at the work of restoration. They'd given thought to the kinds of native grasses and wildflowers to be used, how some dense nesting-cover was needed here, some space there, some snow-free areas planted with fruit-bearers like buffaloberry. Hidden in the icy drizzle, science was at work, and it was good to know it was there.

I was about ready to pick up speed and leave, but Stop Number Five was on the National Register of Historic Places and I couldn't imagine what, in this world, that could be. Once again I turned onto a field road, bumping over half-frozen ridges of mud while I read the brochure, the home ahead built in the "Russia Ukraine style" around 1900 by Daniel Winter, a German Russian settler, and suddenly there it was. A clump of small trees half around it for protection, the Winter House was a small, two-room structure, its wooden roof collapsing inward, its walls that mixture of clay and straw sometimes called puddled straw, the abode of the north.

I stepped in, marveling at the thick walls, a good two feet, and how earth and water and wisps of threshed stalks could withstand the snow and winds of ninety-five Dakota winters, spring melts, blasting summers. It would be cooler in the heat than a frame building and perhaps warmer in winter, but it was still small—I stepped it off at about 18 by 26 feet—and I tried to imagine it as my house, but cramped with how many other family members? And how far away from any others in the prairie solitude?

I thought of where we lived—apartments, old houses, new subdivisions, pits in the earth, the detritus retreats of Caddis fly—and what happened to us where we lived and after we went away. Putting my hand out, I felt the chill of the wall. This was it, my last stop, unplanned and unforeseen. I'd followed the current of a river from spring almost beyond fall through an ordinary countryside, finding a mystery here, a tension there, the truth a combination of harmony and conflict that made me almost helpless. Heraclitus went in search of himself, or at least Plutarch said that he did, and John Neihardt claimed, after his rough Missouri trip at the beginning of what we call the century, that he had discovered another part of himself. I wasn't sure I'd found myself—only Everything Else.

A mile or so away the Sheyenne—moving with the most delicate and powerful currents and countercurrents past our lives of fort and village, church and cemetery—began over and over with complete thoughtlessness, its last waters a mixture of everything since its beginning. Winter was setting in to freeze it over, to form the shell of ice that the spring flood would lift up into the elms, a high-water mark we could see as we drove over our nearest bridge, and then that ice melting back.

I'd seen the same patterns the way one can find the same design in a leaf or tree or central nervous system. I'd felt the same rhythms of rise and fall, the heartbeat of a lake, the seasonal pulse of rivers, the rains that steadily lured us and unpredictably destroyed us, the charts of wheat prices and the demographics of small towns, our places, our fates. To believe, as had the Cheyenne, that the past was simultaneous with the present seemed, in this landscape, completely and utterly reasonable.

Our conditions, South Dakota poet John Milton says, have caused us "to linger a little longer than other regions in a kind of frontier condition." It was this space in which we lived that set the limits to how large we could feel and how little, how powerful, over the land and how impotent against it. It was this combination of rhythms inside this space that gave those who lived along a river, and that was all of us, a feeling for the irreconcilable movements of change and stability, a dynamic equilibrium. Could we here, as Dakotans sometimes thought, prove how America was going to be able to survive in the next century? Did we, as John Milton thought, have the opportunity "of linking the past with the future, of carrying the old values over into the new ones"? We had at least a chance. If, he warned, "we could learn our lesson fast enough."

The present held the past in one way and the future in another and this was the lesson of water and earth and time and of our lives, all changed, nothing changed, all to *be* changed. I'd come to understand from one year's journey why it sometimes seemed foolish to call a thing a river—its nature so dependent on everything before, after, around, and ahead of it, so full of growth and limitation that it couldn't carry a single name. And I understood why it sometimes seemed foolish not to call everything a river.

I crouched down in a corner of the Winter House, its monumental walls melting around a small emptiness, a first home slowly eroding away. The air outside carried a chill of glacier but I didn't want to leave. This was, after all, the last house, the last winter, the last of the beginning of the river. The moment I started to leave it, I'd start to leave everything. I'd wait until it got too cold, I told myself, settling down against the wall. I wondered how long that would take.

endnotes

PREFACE

All references to Thom McGrath's poetry in this book come from *Letter to an Imaginary Friend, Parts I and II* (Swallow Press, Chicago, IL: 1970) and *Parts III and IV* (Copper Canyon Press, Port Townsend, WA: 1985)

CHAPTER ONE—
AROUND THE BEGINNING IN SHERIDAN COUNTY

My main source for regional geological information throughout this book is State Geologist John P. Bluemle's *The Face of North Dakota* (Ed. Series 21, North Dakota Geological Survey, Bismarck, ND: 1991) as well as his *Geology and Ground Water Resources* for each county.

The standard history is Elwyn Robinson's *A History of North Dakota* (Univ. of Nebraska Press, Lincoln: 1966). For all information about town origins, names, and dates, I'm indebted to Douglas Wick's *North Dakota Place Names* (Hedemarken Collectibles, Bismarck, ND: 1988). General information and population numbers usually come from the *North Dakota Blue Book* (Secretary of State Alvin Jaeger, Bismarck, ND: 1995).

For much of Sheridan's history, I'm indebted to Jim Wills's *Sheridan County Heritage Book: A Centennial Project* (McClusky, ND: 1989).

CHAPTER TWO—
CONTINENTAL DIVIDE: LOOKING BACK ACROSS THE YEARS

Wells County history is detailed in Walter Spokesfield's *The History of Wells County and Its Pioneers* (Valley City, ND: 1929) and the more recent compilation by Barbara Levorsen in *The Quiet Conquest: History of Wells County* (Hawley Herald, Hawley, MN: 1974).

The discussion of continental drift and plate tectonics derives from Robert Dott Jr. and Roger Batten's *Evolution of the Earth* (McGraw-Hill, New York City, NY: 1976), William Glen's *Continental Drift and Plate Tectonics* (Merrill, Columbus, OH: 1975), Carl Seyfert's *The Encyclopedia of Structural Geology and Plate Tectonics* (Van Nostrand Reinhold, New York City, NY: 1987), and Raymond Siever's article, "The Dynamic Earth," *Scientific American* (vol. 249, no. 3, Sept. 1983).

John Boyle's "Notes from an Agricultural Field Trip Across North Dakota (1916)" originally appeared in *The Quarterly Journal of the University of North Dakota* (Jan. 1917) but is reprinted in the Buffalo Commons Issue of *North Dakota Quarterly* (Fall 1996, vol. 63, no. 4).

Elizabeth Hampsten's "The Nehers and the Martins in North Dakota, 1909–1911," is found in *Far From Home: Families of the Westward Journey,* ed. Schlissel, Gibbens, and Hampsten (Schocken Books, New York City, NY: 1989). Lois Phillips Hudson's observation is taken from *Reapers of the Dust: A Prairie Chronicle* (Minnesota Historical Society Press, St. Paul, MN: 1984).

Other books referred to or quoted from are O. E. Rolvaag's *Their Fathers' God* (Harper & Brothers, New York City, NY: 1931), Jonathan Raban's *Badland: An American Romance* (Random House, New York City, NY: 1996), Editor L. Brent Bohlke's *Willa Cather in Person: Interviews, Speeches, and Letters* (Univ. of Neb. Press, Lincoln, NE: 1986), and William R. Conte's privately printed manuscript of family history, *The Johnsons of North Dakota* (N.p., Olympia, WA: 1991).

CHAPTER THREE: FAITH IN NORTH DAKOTA

The O. E. Rolvaag trilogy of novels referred to here and elsewhere are *Giants in the Earth* (Harper & Brothers, New York City, NY: 1927), *Peder Victorious* (Harper & Brothers, New York City, NY: 1929), and *Their Fathers' God* (Harper & Brothers, New York City, NY: 1931). My reading of Rolvaag was substantially helped by Harold P. Simonson's *Prairies Within: The Tragic Trilogy of Ole Rolvaag* (Univ. of Washington Press, Seattle, WA: 1987). An idea of the theological issues involved was gained from W. Kent Gilbert's *Commitment to Unity: A History of the Lutheran Church in America* (Fortress Press, Philadelphia, PA: 1988) and Theodore Tappert's *Lutheran Confessional Theology in America, 1840–1880* (Oxford Univ. Press, NY: 1972).

A good source for Eddy County history is *A Century of Sowers, A Harvest of Heritage* (Eddy County Centennial Historical Committee, New Rockford, ND: 1983). The personal history of Emil Gunsch is found in *Family Homestead Reflections* (Vantage Press, New York City, NY: 1986) and information on Rachel Calof comes from J. Sanford Rikoon's *Rachel Calof's Story: Jewish Homesteader on the Northern Plains* (Indiana Univ. Press, Bloomington, IN: 1995). General information on the distribution of immigration is presented in William C. Sherman's *Prairie Mosaic: An Ethnic Atlas of Rural North Dakota* (North Dakota Institute for Regional Studies, Fargo, ND: 1983) as well as Sherman and Thorson's *Plains Folk: North Dakota's Ethnic History* (North Dakota Institute for Regional Studies, Fargo, ND: 1988).

Kathleen Norris's ideas come from *Dakota: A Spiritual Geography* (Ticknow & Fields, New York City, NY: 1993).

CHAPTER FOUR—SPIRIT LAKE, SPIRIT HEART

Contemporary details of and attitudes toward the Sioux Uprising are found in Charles S. Bryant's *A History of the Great Massacre by the Sioux Indians in Minnesota* (Rickey & Carroll, Cincinnati, OH: 1864), Issac Heard's *History of the Sioux War* (Harper and Bros. New York City, NY: 1863), William Marshall's *Journal of Military Expedition Against the Sioux Indians from Camp Pope in the Summer of 1863* (Original in the manuscript division of the Minnesota Historical Society), and Harriet Bishop McConkey's *Dakota War Whoop: Or Indian Massacres and War in Minnesota of 1862–4* (Moses' Press, St. Paul. MN: 1864).

Material regarding the Devils Lake Reservation and Fort Totten was derived from Roy W. Meyer's *History of the Santee Sioux: United States Indian Policy on Trial* (Univ. of Nebraska Press, Lincoln, NE: 1967), Mary Jane Schneider's *North Dakota Indians: An Introduction* (Kendall-Hunt, Dubuque, IA: 1986), Harold Schunk's *History of Fort Totten* (U.S. Dept. of Interior, Bureau of Indian Affairs, Belcourt, ND: 1937), and Charles Noyer's "The History of Fort Totten" in *Collections of the State Historical Society of North Dakota,* ed. O. G. Libby (Bismarck, ND: 1910). Additional material came from Kurt Schweigert's *Initial Settlement Patterns in the Vicinity of Devils Lake, North Dakota* (M.A. Thesis, Univ. of North Dakota, Grand Forks, ND: 1981) and R. T. Young's *The Life of Devils Lake North Dakota* (North Dakota Biological Station, Devils Lake, ND: 1924).

The John Collier book referred to is his famous *Indians of the Americas* (W. W. Norton, New York City, NY: 1947). All news commentaries cited here and throughout the book, unless credited elsewhere, are from the *Grand Forks Herald* or *North Dakota Weekly*, also published at the time by the *Herald*.

CHAPTER FIVE—
WITH HERACLITUS AND NICOLLET ON THE SHEYENNE

My main source for information on Nicollet is Edmund and Martha Bray's *Joseph N. Nicollet on the Plains and Prairies* (Minn. Historical Society

Press, Minneapolis, MN: 1976) and Martha Bray's *Joseph Nicollet and His Map* (American Philosophical Society, Philadelphia, PA: 1980). John Charles Frémont's perspective comes from Allan Nevis's edition of Frémont's *Narration of Exploration and Adventure* (Longmans, Green & Co., New York City, NY: 1956), and I gained information on the Fisk expeditions from Helen White's *Ho for the Gold Fields: Northern Overland Wagon Trains of the 1860s* (Minnesota Historical Society, St. Paul, MN: 1966).

The most helpful discussions of Heraclitus for me were T. M. Robinson's *Heraclitus: Fragments, a Text and Translation* (Univ. of Toronto Press, Toronto: 1987), Charles Kahn's *The Art and Thought of Heraclitus: An Edition of the Fragments with Translation and Commentary* (Cambridge University Press, New York City, NY: 1979), and Philip Wheelwright's *Heraclitus* (Princeton Univ. Press, Princeton, NJ: 1959).

CHAPTER SIX—LOST IN THE BOTTOMLANDS

Roy Johnson's description of early steamboating is quoted from his "Frontier Times" article for the Clay County Historical Society, reprinted in *Red River Review* (Fargo, March 1995).

References to other experiences with rivers are Henry David Thoreau's *A Week on the Concord and Merrimac Rivers* (Houghton, Mifflin, New York City, NY: 1893), Henry Dyke's *Little Rivers; A Book of Essays in Profitable Idleness* (Charles Scribner's Sons, New York City, NY: 1901), John Neihardt's *The River and I* (Univ. of Neb. Press, Lincoln: 1968), and Mark Twain's *Life on the Mississippi* (Harper, New York City, NY: 1951).

For thinking about Thoreau, I'm indebted to Linck Johnson's *Thoreau's Complex Weave: The Writing of a Week on the Concord and Merrimac Rivers with the Text of the First Draft* (Bibliographical Society of the Univ. of Virginia, Charlottesville, VA: 1985).

Beside gaining direct information from Univ. of North Dakota professor Frank Beaver, I had help in understanding water from Petts and Foster's *Rivers and Landscape* (Edward Arnold, London: 1985), Litton and Tetlow's *Water and Landscape: An Aesthetic Overview of the Role of*

Water in the Landscape (Report to the National Water Commission, Water Information Center, Port Washington, NY: 1974), and especially Marie Morisawa's *Streams: Their Dynamics and Morphology* (McGraw-Hill, New York City, NY: 1968).

The reference to Agassiz is from Edward Lurie's treatment in *Louis Agassiz: A Life in Science* (University of Chicago Press, Chicago: 1960).

CHAPTER SEVEN—FOLLOWING GENERAL SIBLEY

Descriptions of the Sibley Expedition are based on the following contemporary accounts: Oscar G. Wall, *Recollections of the Sioux Massacre with a Historical Sketch of the Sibley Expedition of 1863* (The Home Printery, Lake City, MN: 1909); Nathaniel West, *The Ancestry, Life, and Times of Hon. Henry Hastings Sibley, LL.D.* (Pioneer Press: St. Paul, MN 1889); William Marshall, "Journal of Military Expedition Against the Sioux Indians" (Manuscript division of the Minnesota Historical Society); Enoch Eastman, "Diary" (*North Dakota Historical Quarterly,* Vol. 1, no. 3); William Clandenning, "Journal" (*North Dakota Historical Quarterly,* Vol. 2, no. 4); and Dana Wright's "The Sibley Trail of 1863," *North Dakota History* (Vol. 2, 1928; Vol. 3, 1946; and Vol. 29, 1962).

The Bryant book, also referred to in Chapter Four, is *A History of the Great Massacre by the Sioux Indians in Minnesota* (Rickey & Carroll, Cincinnati, OH: 1864). Other racial references here are based on Oscar Handlin's *Race and Nationality in American Life* (Atlantic Little Brown and Co., Boston: 1948, 1957) and Henry Pratt Fairchild's *The Melting-Pot Mistake* (Little Brown and Co., Boston: 1926).

CHAPTER EIGHT—AT THE FORT, AT THE VILLAGE

Lowell Goodman's report is *The Economic Health of North Dakota* (LRG Properties Ltd. with the Univ. of North Dakota Alumni Association, Grand Forks, ND: 1996). Passages of Thomas McGrath's poetry come from Parts I and II of *Letters to an Imaginary Friend* (Swallow Press, Chicago, IL: 1970).

References to Cheyenne history and stories come from Tristram Coffin's *Indian Tales of North Americas* (American Folklore Society, Philadelphia, PA: 1961), George Bird Grinnel's *The Cheyenne Indians: Their History and Ways of Life* (Yale University Press, New Haven, CT: 1923), Tom Weist's *A History of the Cheyenne People* (Montana Council for Indian Education, Billings, MT: undated), John Moore's *The Cheyenne Nation: A Social and Demographic History* (Univ. of Nebraska Press, Lincoln, NE: 1987), and his later *The Cheyenne* (Blackwell Publishers, Cambridge MA: 1996).

The reference to Marie Sandoz is her poignant *Cheyenne Autumn* (Avon Books, New York City, NY: 1964), with additional reference to John H. Stands in Timber's *Cheyenne Memories,* with the assistance of Robert Utley (Univ. of Neb. Press, Lincoln, NE: 1967). My information on the site of the Cheyenne village near Lisbon is gathered from W. Raymond Wood's *Biesterfeldt: A Post-Contact Coalescent Site on the Northeastern Plains* (Smithsonian Press, Washington, DC: 1971).

CHAPTER NINE—PAST AND FUTURE IN THE GRASSLANDS

Information on Sheyenne Township comes from Mrs. Jorgen Haugen's *The History of Sheyenne Township* (Richland County Historical Society, Wahpeton, ND: 1974) and the Sheyenne Historical Society's *Our Heritage: Sheyenne Area, 1883–1983* (Altona, Manitoba: 1980).

References for the first Buffalo Commons discussions are to Deborah and Frank Popper's "The Great Plains: From Dust to Dust" (*Planning* 53, Dec. 1987) and Jon Margolis's "The Reopening of the Frontier" (*The New York Times Magazine,* Oct. 15, 1995). Their next major presentation and the responses to it are found in *Forum for Applied Research and Public Policy* (Winter 1994, vol. 9, no. 4). This includes the Poppers' "Great Plains: Checkered Past, Hopeful Future," John C. Shepard's "Grassroots Response form the Great Plains," Jay Swisher's "South Dakotans Dig in, Seek to Stay on Plains," Dave Egan and Bill Whitney's "Buffalo Commons: Model or Metaphor?," and Vine Deloria Jr.'s "Renewal and Revival on the Great Plains."

Additional information and opinions are found in the "Buffalo Commons Issue" of the *North Dakota Quarterly* (vol. 63, no. 4, Fall 1996), including Kathleen Norris's "Miles upon Miles" and Rick Watson's "Where the Buffalo Roam: An Interview with Larry Woiwode."

CHAPTER TEN—RIVER END: THE BONANZA VALLEY

Information and opinions about the Red River Valley are found in Hiram Drache's *The Challenge of the Prairie: Life and Times of Red River Pioneers* (North Dakota Institute for Regional Studies, Fargo: 1970) and his *The Day of the Bonanza* (North Dakota Institute for Regional Studies, Fargo: 1984). Rich and helpful resources include Stan Murray's *The Valley Comes of Age: A History of Agriculture in the Valley of the Red River of the North, 1812–1920* (North Dakota Institute for Regional Studies, Fargo: 1967) and Nancy Hanson's *Heart of the Prairie* (North Dakota Centennial Series, Vol. 3, Dakota Graphic Society, 1985).

Mary Dodge Woodward's experiences are found in *The Checkered Years*, edited by Mary Cowdrey (The Caxton Printers, Caldwell, ID: 1937). For information on Sitting Bull here and elsewhere I depended on Robert Utley's *The Lance and the Shield: The Life and Times of Sitting Bull* (Henry Holt & Co, New York City, NY: 1993).

CHAPTER ELEVEN—THE WINTER HOUSES

John Scott's 1923 reminiscence is reprinted in the Buffalo Commons issue of the *North Dakota Quarterly* (Vol. 63, no. 4, Fall 1996). The major government report referred to is *The Future of the Great Plains: Report of the Great Plains Committee* (Gov. Printing Office, Washington, DC: Dec. 1936) but the "Summary Foreword" from which I quote is reprinted in *Mississippi Valley Historical Review* (Mississippi Valley Historical Association, Urbana, IL), 49–68.

Quoted comments on Dakota character come from David Danbom's "North Dakota: The Most Midwestern State" in *Heartland: Comparative*

Histories of the Midwestern States, ed. James Madison (Indiana University Press, Bloomington, IN: 1988); John Milton's "The Dakota Image" (*South Dakota Review,* Autumn 1970); Kathleen Norris's *Dakota: A Spiritual Geography* ((Ticknow & Fields, New York City, NY: 1993); and an interview with Larry Woiwode by Rick Watson, "Where the Buffalo Roam" (*North Dakota Quarterly*, Fall 1996).

Information on the Columbian Exposition is based on Reid Badger's *The Great American Fair: The World's Columbian Exposition and American Culture* (Nelson Hall, Chicago: 1970). The Halsey quotation is from Francis Halsey's *Great Epochs in American History* (Funk and Wagnalls, New York City, NY: 1912).

My thoughts about the frontier and the west were influenced by Robert Athearn's *The Mythic West in Twentieth-Century America* (Univ. Press of Kansas, Lawrence, KS: 1986) and especially Harold Simonson's *Beyond the Frontier* (Texas Christian Univ. Press, Fort Worth, TX: 1989). I also learned from the essays in editor Mohan Wali's *Prairie: A Multiple View* (Univ. of North Dakota Press, Grand Forks, ND: 1975).

Not referred to but certainly important to this subject are Walter Prescott Webb's *The Great Plains* (Grosset & Dunlap, New York City, NY: 1931) and Ian Frazier's *Great Plains* (Farrar, Straus, & Giroux, New York City, NY: 1989).